CHILDREN'S BOOKS

THIS CANADIAN SCOUT HANDBOOK BELONGS TO

_____

A MEMBER OF THE

_____

PATROL OF THE

_____

TROOP, WHICH MEETS AT

_____
Place

ON _____ FROM _____ TO _____
Day   Time   Time

Place photo of your patrol here

CANADIAN SCOUT HANDBOOK

SCOUTS CANADA

PUBLISHED BY
SCOUTS CANADA
NATIONAL OFFICE

www.scouts.ca

ISBN # 978-1-926557-37-3   Catalogue # 20-467/2009

Printed in Canada

IMPORTANT NAMES   PHONE   E-MAIL

Patrol Leader

Assistant Patrol Leader

Patrol Member

Patrol Member

Patrol Member

Patrol Member

Patrol Member

Patrol Counsellor

Troop Scouter

Other

Other

Other

Other

TABLE OF CONTENTS

SCOUTING IS

- ◎ FRIENDSHIP
- ◎ ACHIEVEMENT
- ◎ ADVENTURE
- ◎ FUN
- ◎ CHALLENGE

WHAT DO YOU EXPECT FROM SCOUTING?

Before you look at any other part of this book, take a few moments to make a list of the kinds of things you'd like to do while you're a Scout. Since this is your list, there are no limits on what you can put in it.

_____

_____

_____

_____

_____

_____

_____

_____

_____

_____

What kinds of activities did you write down? Perhaps a lot of the ideas you listed were about things you wanted to do outdoors — activities like camping, hiking, canoeing, sailing, and snowshoeing. You might have thought about sports such as archery, fishing, cross-country skiing, or orienteering. Maybe you wanted to play games or learn how to do new things such as camp cooking. And maybe your wishes included finding some other kids who share your hobbies or other interests.

As a Scout, you will have opportunities to do all these things, and more! What's most exciting about being a Scout is that you will constantly discover new activities you hadn't even thought of trying.

Fun is likely something you want from Scouting, and you'll get plenty of it in different forms. You'll have noisy fun doing things like playing wide games or building and flying kites. Activities such as swimming, tobogganing, or horseback riding will offer lots of physical fun. You'll have mental fun figuring out how to do a new skill like making a rope or cooking without pots and pans. Sometimes you'll have quiet fun, such as when you're sitting by yourself next to a lake and you hear the lonely cry of a loon, or when you're winter camping and a Canadian Blue Jay noiselessly glides into a nearby tree to keep you company.

Friendship will come in different ways, too. To beginwith, you probably already know several kids who are

Scouts. Doing things with other Scouts will help you make new friends. When you spend several hours in a canoe with someone you don't know very well, you get to know each other a lot better, especially if the two of you have to portage the canoe any distance. Camporees and jamborees give you chances to meet more people who may become friends. Sometimes you won't get to meet Scouts face-to-face, but you can talk to them by Ham radio, or become pen pals — friends by mail. You'll also meet adults in Scouting who will become your friends.

Adventure is a constant part of Scouting. The out-of-doors is where a lot of Scouting happens, and it offers many opportunities for adventure. Whether you're building a snow hut, stalking animals in a forest, running through an orienteering course, or practicing how to search for a lost person in the woods, you'll find adventures of many kinds awaiting you. You may have the opportunity to board a plane and fly off

to a jamboree adventure in
another province or country.
You could be part of
a wilderness canoe
expedition, a
camping/cycling tour,
or an extended cruise
through a series
of lakes.

Challenge will face you
whenever you try something
you haven't done before.
Challenges are both physical and
mental. If you don't know how to swim, the challenge
lies both in the learning and perhaps, in getting over
your fear of the water. If you're a good summer camper, challenge comes when you take your skill and add
to it by moving on to winter camping. Accepting a challenge is an important way for you to grow as a person.
And having good Scouting friends makes taking on
a new challenge just a little bit easier.

Achievement is what you will feel when you've
successfully tackled an adventure or mastered new
knowledge or a new skill. A sense of achievement
makes you feel good about yourself. Perhaps you just
learned a new swimming stroke or a new water rescue
method, or you completed a 25 km hike. Maybe you
took part in a Scoutrees project and can look with pride
at what you've done. Before you started, you stood on
the edge of a bare field. Now it is dotted with seedlings

which, in a few years, will grow into a tall forest. The various badges and awards in the Scout program are ways of publicly recognizing your achievements in many areas of your life, both physical and mental.

YOU IN THE PATROL AND TROOP

As a Scout, you will sometimes do things completely on your own. Most often though, you will take part in activities with other Scouts as part of a group or team that stays together. That semi-permanent group is called a patrol. Patrols normally have five to eight Scouts. A number of patrols make up a Scout troop.

Different troops organize their patrols in differ-ent ways. In some troops, each patrol is made up of Scouts who are about the same age or in the same grades at school. In others, patrols have a mix of older and young-er Scouts.

DID YOU KNOW SCOUTREES was officially launched on May 9, 1974, by His Excellency, Governor General Jules Leger, the Chief Scout of Canada?

Each arrangement has its advantages and disadvantages. What works for one troop may not for another; as a troop changes with time, its members may have to consider reorganizing its patrols.

Patrols are led by one Scout called the **Patrol Leader**. The patrol leader, often called simply the PL, is normally elected by fellow patrol members. When choosing your patrol leader, you need to consider carefully not just each candidate's popularity, but which Scout will make the best leader. The patrol decides how long the PL remains as PL. For example, it might be six months or one year.

Once you have elected someone to be PL, you need to help your leader all you can to do the very best job possible. The *Patrol Leader's Handbook* will also help.

The PL has a helper called an assistant patrol leader or APL. It is usually the PL's right to choose an APL, but a wise PL will consult the other members of the patrol before deciding. Good PLs don't just select their best friend; they choose the Scout who will be the best leader of the patrol when the PL can't be there.

Just because a patrol has a PL and an APL, doesn't mean that these two Scouts must always lead everything. In the best patrols, the needs of a particular situation determine who provides the leadership.

Let's suppose the patrol is working on a particular badge, such as the Canoeing Badge. None of the other Scouts have ever been in a canoe, but you have already completed several canoe expeditions. Obviously, this is a time when the patrol can use your expertise and experience. A patrol that uses each of its members' skills and abilities to the fullest will have good esprit de corps, or patrol spirit.

Your patrol will have an adult advisor called a **Patrol Counsellor**. The patrol has a lot of responsibility for planning what it is going to do and carrying out those plans. Your Patrol Counsellor will guide you. Normally, he or she will say "no" to something only when what you want to do is either contrary to Scouting's Principles or unsafe.

One of your adult leaders is known as the **Troop Scouter**. While your Patrol Counsellor usually works just with your patrol, the Troop Scouter has overall responsibility for all the patrols in the troop. Sometimes, the Troop Scouter may be a Patrol Counsellor as well. All of the adult leaders in your Scout troop are volunteers. You'll find that many of them were Scouts when they were your age, and they liked Scouting so much that they came back as leaders.

How do you address your adult leaders when you want to talk to them? Some may ask you to call them by their last name with the title "Mr." or "Scouter" put in front of it (e.g. Mr. Jones or Scouter Jones). Others might prefer you to use their first name with the term "Scouter" before it e.g. Scouter Rob). Still others may have a special Scouting name, such as "Greybeard", "Badger", or "Skink."

After you've known your Troop Scouter or Patrol Counsellor for some time, you may come up with a name you think suits the person. (One Patrol Counsellor got the Name "Ogre-Belly" from his patrol after a jamboree.) Just remember, before you give your Patrol Counsellor a new name, make sure you give it because you are fond of your Scouter and think it's a name he or she wants to "wear."

Your Troop Scouter, Patrol Counsellor, and fellow Scouts will be of great help to you when you want to earn various badges and awards in the Scout program, but sometimes nobody in the troop will have the skills or knowledge you need. When that happens, you'll have to go outside the troop to find a resource person who has the specialized information. Start with parents, neighbours, and teachers. You'll find they're very helpful and willing to share their expertise.

PATROL EMBLEM

When Lord Robert Baden-Powell, the founder of Scouting, held his first experimental Scout camp on **Brownsea Island** from August 1-8, 1907, he organized the 21 boys who attended into four patrols. Each patrol was named for a mammal or bird. The original four patrols were

DID YOU KNOW CANADA HAS HOSTED TWO WORLD JAMBOREES: The first was in 1955 at Niagara-on-the-Lake, and the second was in 1983 at Kananaskis, Alberta?

the Wolves, the Bulls, the Curlews, and the Ravens.

As a new Scout, you may become a member of a patrol that already has a name. If, however, you are in a brand new patrol, you and the other patrol members will get to choose your patrol's name. While you can pick any name you wish, you will probably want to find a name that tells others what type of Scouts you want to be now and in the years to come. You'll also wear an emblem on your tan uniform to show others that you are a member of a particular patrol.

Your patrol can design its own emblem, but many patrols decide to choose their patrol name from among the birds and mammals in the "Wildlife Crest Series." These crests, represent animals that are either seasonal or permanent residents of Canada.

Your patrol might take a bird's name such as owl, hawk, or eagle. You could be the fox, wolf, or polar bear patrol. Thinking of the qualities associated with certain birds and mammals may help you select a name. For example, when you hear the words "grizzly" or "Canada goose", what qualities come to mind?

My patrol is called the _____
This is a good name for us because _____
_____

THE PATROL AND TROOP IN ACTION

Your patrol and troop will have two main kinds of meetings: planning and activity meetings.

When the patrol gets together to discuss plans for future activities, the meetings are called patrol meetings. The patrol can hold these meetings apart from your regular troop meeting time in the home of one of the patrol members. Perhaps your patrol has even created or built its own special meeting place. Terrific!

Usually there are specific reasons for calling a patrol meeting. Perhaps the patrol wants to decide which badge its members are going to earn next, and needs everyone to have a say in making the decision.

Once you've all chosen a badge, the patrol may want to decide which options within the badge requirements it is going to follow.

Maybe you have a camp or hike coming up, and the patrol has to draw up a menu to decide who is going to buy the food, and who is going to prepare the patrol equipment.

Maybe the patrol just wants to do some long-range planning, and needs members to say what they would like to see the patrol do in the next three to six months. The patrol's job is then to take everyone's idea and work out a plan that gives each member at least some preferred activities. The PL's job in the patrol meeting is to coordinate the meeting. Someone needs to make a written record of the major decisions the patrol makes so you all can keep track of who has agreed to do what.

Patrol meetings don't always have to be formal. They can be called whenever a patrol has a problem to solve. Suppose you're on a bike hike. You'd planned to go 50 km, but extremely strong winds slowed you down. The PL might quickly call a patrol meeting to decide whether or not the patrol wants to modify its original plans because of the unexpected circumstances.

A patrol meeting is a time for everyone's opinions to be heard. Be prepared to volunteer your own thoughts. If you notice that some of your patrol members aren't contributing, encourage them to give their ideas. The more ideas you have, the better decisions you can make.

Patrol meetings are also a time to share feelings. Perhaps you aren't happy being in your patrol. Share this information with other patrol members. Perhaps the patrol needs to begin to behave in a different way towards you, or possibly you might be happier if you were a member of another patrol.

The other major planning meeting is the **Court of Honour**. This meeting coordinates the plans of the patrols and also makes short- and long-term plans for the entire troop. For example, the Court of Honour might decide when and where the next troop camp will be held, and what its theme will be. As well, the

Court of Honour could say which patrols will serve as the **Service Patrol** at troop meetings to take care of such tasks as preparing the flag for flag break, and cleaning up after the meeting.

Membership in the Court of Honour is usually limited to one representative from each patrol — most often the patrol leader. In very small troops, assistant patrol leaders may also be members; the Troop Scouter usually is the Court's resource person. Your representative is responsible for taking your patrol's ideas to the Court of Honour.

A good patrol leader represents the interests of the entire patrol at the Court of Honour, not just personal interests. Suppose all the patrols in the troop agreed they wanted to go bowling, but couldn't decide if it should be five or ten pin. In your patrol meeting, your patrol decided it preferred five pin bowling, but your PL wanted ten pin. At the Court of Honour, the PL's responsibility is to report the patrol's preference for five pin.

The PL not only takes information to the Court of Honour, but also reports back to the patrol meeting any Court of Honour decisions that affect the patrol.

It is the responsibility of each member of this Court of Honour to:

1. Set a good example in living the Scout Promise and Law;
2. Uphold the honour and traditions of this troop;
3. Consider the wishes of the patrol before personal wishes;
4. Be fair and just when making all judgments;
5. Abide cheerfully by the decisions of the majority;
6. Help the Troop Scouter with the operation of the troop;
7. Respect the secrecy of Court of Honour discussions when appropriate.

Activity meetings happen both at the patrol and troop level. Troops vary in how often they meet as a whole troop. Some troops hold evening troop meetings every week in an outdoor setting, such as a park or campground. Other troops meet indoors in a large meeting space, like a school gym or community club, and then hold part of their meetings outside. As well

as a time to play games and learn new things, troop meetings offer occasions for ceremonies to recognize Scouts for earning various Scout awards.

Through the planning of the Patrols in Council and Court of Honour, many troops hold at least some form of major outdoor expedition, such as a camp, hike, cruise, or canoeing trip every month of the year. Other troops also hold a long-term camp, hike, cruise, or canoe trip during the summer.

Patrol meetings are fun times. Almost anywhere can be a patrol meeting place. Here's what you'll find: the more often your patrol meets, the better you'll get to know everyone, the more fun you'll have, and the greater the patrol spirit will be.

You can use patrol meetings to practise skills like foil cooking, or to work on patrol projects. Patrol meetings also give you extra opportunities to work on badges. You can also use patrol meetings just to get together and spend time with each other. Some patrols plan and hold outdoor activities or events in addition to those conducted by the troop.

While your Patrol Counsellor does not have to be at every one of your patrol meetings, tell him or her when you're going to hold them. This lets Scouters plan their own schedules so they're available if you need them.

YOUTH NETWORKS

Youth Networks have been established at all levels of Scouting to provide input on important issues. Your patrol/troop sets the basis for this network and should be involved in a larger network of youth periodically. Find out more from your patrol leader or visit the National Youth Committee on Scouts Canada's web site, www.scouts.ca.

LOOKING LIKE A SCOUT

Your **uniform** is one way of identifying you as a member of the world's largest youth organization.

The choice of uniform for all occasions is made by the individual and their family.

Scouts have several uniform options available for everyday outdoor program activities. Any of these options are deemed acceptable for Scouting activities.

DID YOU KNOW THE SASKATCHEWAN SCOUT (1916) was one of the first Scouting papers produced in Canada. It had a circulation of 1600 copies?

Show pride in your uniform and yourself by keeping it clean, pressed, and in good repair.

The diagram on page 124 shows where you wear the various Scout badges and awards on the tan shirt/ scout sash.

SEA SCOUTS

Sea Scouts, identified by the anchor on their epaulets, are part of the Scout section, and share the same Promise and Law. One way to think about Sea Scouts is that they practise their Scouting afloat on Canada's oceans, lakes and rivers. While a Sea Scout troop follows the core Scout program, a lot of the troop's activities will take place on, or near, water.

A Sea Scout troop uses sailing terminology when organizing itself. The troop is called "the ship's company"; patrols are called "boat crews"; patrol leaders are referred to as "coxswains"; and so on. Formations and ceremonies, such as flag break, also follow nautical practices.

Sea Scouts work to earn the same badges as other Scouts.

What is a JOTA (pronounced Jaw-ta)? The letters stand for Jamboree on the Air, an event that happens each year on the third weekend in October. Since 1958, Scouts around the world have been using JOTA to talk to each other through the use of amateur radio stations.

If you and your patrol haven't been involved in a JOTA before, why not start making plans now? You don't have to be a Ham — an amateur radio operator — to do it. The first step is to contact one of your local amateur radio operators. The easiest way to find one is to look around your neighbourhood for a large, strange-looking antenna.

Many Hams will invite Scouts to their "shacks" (the word Hams use for their home radio stations) for the JOTA. If you can't locate any antennas, talk to the staff at a local radio dealer's store. They should be able to find the names of amateur radio clubs in your area.

DID YOU KNOW THE LARGEST EVER GATHERING of Canadian Scouts was at the 1981 Canadian Jamboree at Kananaskis, Alberta. About 20,000 attended.

Perhaps you can combine JOTA with a weekend camp. Ask a Ham operator to bring his or her mobile station to your campsite. That way, one of your patrol projects could involve building a tall tower or flagpole for the radio's antenna. Bring along a world map or globe so you can "see" the countries you're talking to on the radio.

After the fun of talking to Scouts in other countries during JOTA, you can have fun exchanging QSL cards with the stations you contact. What is a

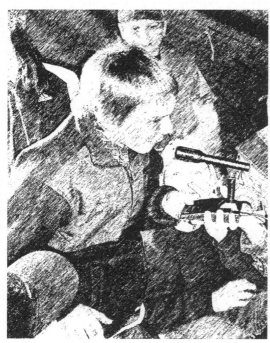

QSL card? It's just a postcard each station sends to other stations it contacts. One side of a JOTA-QSL card usually carries a design linked to JOTA or Scouting, while the other side provides details of the contact, including the station's call sign. Perhaps, as part of your Artist Challenge Badge, you can design your own special JOTA-QSL cards!

A useful starting point in your JOTA planning is the booklet, *Jamboree on the Air: How Canadians Can Participate.* Ask your Patrol Counsellor to get a copy from the local Scout office or find it on Scouts Canada's web site, www.scouts.ca.

For those with Internet access, JOTI (Jamboree on the Internet) is run in the same manner. Check out the details at: www.scout.org.

SCOUTREES FOR CANADA

Since 1973, Canadian Scouting members have planted more than 70 million tree seedlings as part of the Scoutrees for Canada program. To understand how many trees that is, if they had planted all of these 70 million trees along the Trans-Canada Highway's 7,699 km length, you would find a tree approximately every 9 cm. coast to coast!

The Scoutrees for Canada project helps reforest Canada and reclaim waste area. You can see that the Scoutrees for Canada symbol is made up of three parts. Can you suggest what each part stands for?

By calling door-to-door in their communities, Scouts collect pledges from people who want to see trees planted in the reforestation area. The money they collect is used in a variety of ways. One special use is the Canadian Scout Brotherhood Fund. Money that goes to the Brotherhood Fund helps support world Scout community development projects.

Examples of the Canadian Scout Brotherhood Fund in action include a grant to Indonesia, where Indonesian Scouts built a fresh water system. Now the Scouts' community has safe water for drinking and other household purposes, such as bathing and washing clothes. In Bolivia, Scouts who were concerned about the local food supply established a rabbit farm to improve nutrition.

As you can see, participation in Scoutrees for Canada doesn't just make Canada a better place to live; it also improves living conditions for others in different parts of the world.

JAMBOREES

A jamboree is an international, national, or provincial gathering of Scouts. It was while Lord Robert Stephenson Smyth Baden-Powell was attending the Imperial Scout Exhibition in England in 1913 that he got the idea for jamborees. The exhibition was Scouting's first full-fledged rally; Scouts from a dozen countries in the British Empire attended. As B.-P. watched the events, he thought, "Why not stage

an international encampment that would promote friendship, encourage outdoor skills, and build citizenship?"

Earlier Scout gatherings had been called rallies and exhibitions, but B.-P. wanted a new name for this new idea. The name he came up with for such a gathering was jamboree. He didn't know exactly what the word meant, but he liked its sound. It had the flavour of the Australian Aboriginal word "coroboree", which meant a gathering, and it captured the idea of Scouts "jammed together" at a large gathering.

The first world jamboree was to be held in 1918 to celebrate Scouting's 10th birthday, but World War I delayed it until 1920. More than 6,000 Scouts from 27 countries attended that premier jamboree, which was held for the first and last time indoors at the Olympia exhibition hall in London, England. There, Scouts put on displays of such things as fire- lighting, gymnastics, and tent pitching. They also held competitions in obstacle races, tug-of-wars, and trek cart racing. At this jamboree they invited B.-P. to become "Chief Scout of the World."

Since then, there have been 20 world jamborees. Canada hosted two of them: the eighth in 1955 at Niagara-on-the-Lake, Ontario, and the 15th in 1983 at Kananaskis, Alberta.

We hope that, during your Scouting adventures, you will have the chance to attend a world jamboree. To get a taste of what a jamboree can be like, talk to your Patrol Counsellor about seeing a video or film that features a world or national jamboree.

CANADIAN JAMBOREES

The first Canadian Jamboree was held July 16-24, 1949, at the Connaught Ranges near Ottawa. The second and third Canadian Jamborees were also held

in Ottawa in 1953 and 1961. There wasn't another Canadian Jamboree until 1977.

Since then, national jamborees, often called CJs, have been held every four years in different locations across Canada. The fourth and seventh CJs were in Prince Edward Island in 1977 and 1989. Guelph,

Ontario, was the site of CJ'85, while the Kananaskis Valley in Alberta welcomed CJ'81 and CJ'93. In
1997, Thunder Bay, Ontario, hosted the jamboree
with Prince Edward Island hosting in 2001. The most
recent Canadian Jamboree was held at Camp Tamara-
couta, Quebec in 2007.

Some provinces hold their own provincial jamborees,
and Scouting areas within provinces often hold large
camps called "camporees." Certainly, while you're a
Scout, you'll have a number of opportunities to attend
jamborees and camporees.

What do you need to do to become a Scout? You need to satisfy your Patrol Leader, or Patrol Counsellor that you know and understand the:

☐ 1. Scout Promise and Law;

☐ 2. Scout Motto and Slogan; and

☐ 3. Scout handshake, salute, and sign, and the reasons Scouts use them.

But there's a fourth requirement.

☐ 4. You must have taken part in at least one Scout activity.

Did you notice the boxes in front of each of the four things you have to know or do to become a Scout? If you've looked ahead in this book, you've seen the same kind of boxes in front of various badge requirements. Why are they there?

As you complete each requirement, your Patrol Counsellor, Troop Scouter, or a resource person will "initial" that requirement. In this way, your *Canadian Scout Handbook* will become your own personal record of your achievements in the Scout troop.

When you have completed the four requirements to become a Scout, you will be invested as a Pioneer Scout. At that ceremony, you will receive the Scout epaulettes or pin that identify you as a member of a worldwide organization.

Let's get on to meeting the requirements of becoming a Scout.

THE SCOUT PROMISE

On my honour
I promise that I will do my best
To do my duty to God and the Queen,
To help other people at all times,
And to carry out the spirit of the Scout Law.

Knowing the Scout Promise and Law means more than just being able to repeat the words from memory. A promise is a statement of something you intend to do. By making the Scout Promise, you are telling your fellow Scouts and the troop leaders that you intend to do certain things as a Scout.

What do you think each part of the Scout Promise means? Write down your thoughts before you read what's written below the lines.

_____

_____

_____

_____

_____

Of the five words in the first part of the promise, did you notice that two of the words ("my" and "I") refer directly to you? You are the one who is voluntarily making the Scout Promise. By doing so, you "own" what's in the Promise. At your investiture ceremony, you will repeat the Scout Promise in front of your fellow Scouts and Scout leaders. Each of them will expect you to live up to what you say you are promising to do.

That I Will Do My Best

_____

_____

_____

_____

_____

There's that word "my" again. How fast can you run the 100 m dash? Right now, the world record is just less than 10 seconds. Can you run that fast? Probably not, and your fellow Scouts and Scout leaders wouldn't

likely expect you to. But, suppose your time was
30 seconds. Would the other Scouts and leaders be
satisfied with your effort? The answer is "yes", if
that effort was really the best effort you could give.
Throughout your Scouting experience, the major
expectation and standard of your performance will
be that you are doing your best.

To Do My Duty To God

_____

_____

_____

_____

How can you do your duty to God? There are many
ways. One of the more obvious is to worship, both
publicly and privately. The way you live can show
others that you are following the teachings of your
faith and God. For example, your efforts in conserving
the natural world both serve God and show your love
for God's creation. Making the best use of the talents
and abilities God has given you also demonstrates that
you are doing your duty to God.

_____

_____

_____

_____

Canada is our country. Canada's original people were the land's first citizens, and the rest of Canada's citizens either came here from other countries or are the children of people who moved here. The Queen is the head of the Commonwealth of Nations of which Canada is a part. In Canada, the Queen is represented by the Governor General.

We can do our duty to our Queen and Canada by acting in ways that show we are good citizens. The flag ceremonies that open and close our Scout meetings are one way to demonstrate our respect for Canada. In fact, something as simple as stopping our bikes at a stop sign shows we love and serve our country because we are obeying the laws of Canada. We also show love for our country by not littering or, better yet, by cleaning up trash in our neighbourhoods.

To help other people at all times

What does "other people" mean? To begin with, it includes females and males, as well as adults and children. It doesn't mean just people who live in Canada, but all people who share this planet with us. We can help them in a variety of ways.

Scouting will give you opportunities to help others, but you don't need to wait. Just look around your home and neighbourhood for things that need doing, and then do them.

And to carry out the spirit of the Scout Law

THE SCOUT LAW

A Scout is:
Helpful and trustworthy,
Kind and cheerful,
Considerate and clean,
Wise in the use of all resources.

If you say you are going "to carry out the spirit of the Scout Law," it means you are going to use what the Scout Law says as a guide to your actions. The Scout Law has seven parts.

What does each part of the Scout Law mean to you? Write down your thoughts before you look at the comments that follow.

A Scout is Helpful

_____

_____

_____

_____

_____

Every day, from the moment you wake up until the time you go to bed, you have unlimited opportunities to help others. Just getting up in the morning on your own, without needing someone to nag you out of bed, is being helpful. More active ways

of being helpful in the morning are to make your bed, prepare breakfast, set the table, do the dishes, and make bag lunches for those who take them to school or work. Look at how helpful you've been, and you've only been up an hour!

You can also be helpful outside the home. Perhaps your community has a "Pitch-In" clean-up campaign you can take part in. Or you might support a recycling program. Maybe you can help an elderly neighbour with heavy parts of the yard work.

In Scouts, you will also have opportunities to learn things like first aid or water rescues that will enable you to give one of the greatest acts of help — saving a life.

A Scout is Trustworthy

_____

_____

_____

_____

_____

To be trustworthy means that you are worthy of other people's trust. Think of the kinds of trust you can be given. If you say you are going to do something, people believe that you will do what you say. If you are trustworthy and you can't complete the job you said you would do, people will know, without being told, that there was a good reason you didn't finish it. To be trustworthy means that parents who ask you to babysit feel secure in knowing they can entrust their child's safety and well-being to you. A trustworthy person is someone other people have confidence in.

A Scout is Kind

_____

_____

_____

_____

To be kind means (in part) to act toward others as you would like them to act toward you. Think of words and actions that hurt you, and try not to say or do those things to others. Similarly, think of words and actions that make you feel good, and try to say and do similar things for others.

A Scout is Cheerful

_____

_____

_____

_____

Being cheerful doesn't mean you always have to walk around with a smile plastered on your face. Not everything you do will be fun, but how you look at what seems to be an unpleasant situation or job may determine exactly how unpleasant it really is.

Let's just suppose you don't like homework. Being grouchy and complaining about the homework and the teacher who gave it to you doesn't help you get it done. Probably you won't laugh while you're doing your homework, but tackling it a little more cheerfully might make it seem just a bit lighter.

And not every hike, camp, canoe trip, or cruise you and your patrol take will have clear skies and warm sunshine. Being cheerful and looking for the fun parts in a situation will make you, and others around you, feel much better.

A Scout is Considerate

When you're being considerate you're looking at things
through someone else's
eyes. For example, suppose
you throw your clothes
every-which-way around
your room when you take
them off to get ready for
bed at night. Are you
being considerate?

If you look at your actions through someone else's
eyes, you'll have the answer. You're expecting
someone else to pick up your discarded clothes
and either hang them up or put them wherever
dirty clothes are supposed to go.

Perhaps every morning, you and somebody else
arrive at the bathroom at just about the same time
and argue about who got there first or who uses all
the hot water. To remedy the situation, you could be
considerate and change your showering time.

Consideration is something to practise within your
family and with all people you meet.

A Scout is Clean

This Scout Law refers to at least two types of "clean": an outer clean and an inner clean. The outer cleanliness applies to the real physical things around you. To obey this Scout Law, a Scout keeps his or her body and possessions (such as clothes and personal living space) clean.

To live up to the inner cleanliness part of this law, a Scout keeps his or her body and mind clean by not using tobacco, alcohol or other drugs, and not using foul language.

A Scout is Wise in the Use of All Resources

What are your resources? Probably the first thing you thought about was the money you get as an allowance, or earn from odd jobs. But you have other resources as well. Anything we can use and anything that helps us get something done is a resource.

This book is a resource because you can use it to help you reach your goals as a Scout. Your family members and friends are resources to you. Your abilities and talents are also resources.

To be wise in the use of all resources means that you don't squander them or use them in ways wasteful or harmful to others. For example, if you want a drink of water and let the tap run for five minutes before you fill your glass, you are not wisely using your resources. The water you let go down the drain is no longer available to others. In addition, now other resources have to be used to handle and treat the waste water you created.

All of us must do our part to use the world's renewable and nonrenewable resources wisely.

THE SCOUT MOTTO

The Scout Motto is **BE PREPARED**.

A motto is a short expression that tells you how to behave. Scouts can prepare themselves for whatever may come their way now and in the future by increasing their knowledge and skill.

If someone is hurt in an accident, your first aid skills will prepare you to respond. Knowing the effects of tobacco, alcohol and other drugs on the mind and body will prepare you to say "no" when people offer these substances to you. Being prepared will help you to react correctly when someone begins to show the symptoms of hypothermia. Being a Scout and doing your best prepares you for life.

THE SCOUT SLOGAN

The Scout Slogan is **DO A GOOD TURN DAILY**. Your daily good deeds can take many forms, but all of them will share at least two qualities in common: you will do them happily, and without thought of receiving any payment in the form of money or praise. In other words, you will do good turns to others simply because you genuinely want to help people. Your daily good turns can help just one person, a few people (such as when you help your parents do the family shopping), or a whole community (such as when you take part in a neighbourhood recycling campaign). Just look around; you'll have no trouble finding opportunities galore for your daily good turn.

THE SCOUT SALUTE

The Scout salute is a sign of respect, courtesy, and friend-ship. You use the salute as a sign of respect when the Canadian flag is "broken" at flag break, or when the flag passes by you in a parade. It's also appropriate to use it when the national anthem is being played. You only make the Scout salute when wearing the full Scout uniform (program activity or formal activity option).

To make the Scout salute, place the three fingers of your right hand as shown in the illustration. Bring your hand smartly up to your head until your forefinger touches your eyebrow with the palm of your hand facing forward. Then bring your hand smoothly down to your side.

THE SCOUT SIGN

To make the Scout sign, raise the three fingers of your right hand as you did for the salute. Hold your arm as shown in the illustration. The three fingers in the Scout salute and sign remind you of the three parts of the Scout Promise. Do you remember what they are? The meeting of your thumb and little finger represents the ties of friendship in Scouting.

You use the Scout sign, rather than the Scout salute, on four occasions.

1. When you are making your Scout Promise;

2. When you are attending the investiture of another Scout;

3. When you are anywhere the Scout Promise is being recited; and

4. When you are not in full uniform.

If you are visiting another country and see someone wearing what you think is a Scout uniform, one way to find out if that person is part of the world wide brotherhood of Scouting is to make the Scout sign. The Scout sign is a universal symbol and, if the person is a Scout, he or she will likely flash the sign back to you.

THE SCOUT HANDSHAKE

Did you every wonder why we shake hands when we meet someone? Offering someone our open hand is a gesture of friendship because it shows the other person our hand is free of weapons. But why do Scouts shake hands with their left hand rather than the right?

Evidently the idea came from a legend B.-P. heard while he was in West Africa. Two neighbouring tribes were bitter enemies and always at war. One of the chiefs decided that the battles were harming both tribes, and needed to stop.

When the opposing armies next confronted each other, the chief who wanted peace dropped his spear and shield, and advanced. Not only was the chief's right hand empty of weapons to attack someone else, but his left hand did not hold a shield he could use to defend himself against the weapons of others.

The defenceless chief said to his enemy, "I come unarmed and hold out my left hand to you as a sign of friendship and trust. We are neighbours and should not live as enemies. From now on we wish to live in peace, and we trust you to do the same and live in peace."

When B.-P. founded Scouts, he thought this gesture of friendship and trust would be an excellent one for Scouts to use. The Scout Handshake is made like a right handshake of greeting, except Scouts use their left hands. Show your friendship by reaching out your left hand and shaking someone else's hand firmly, but warmly.

GETTING INVESTED

Once you satisfy your Troop Scouter or Patrol Counsellor that you have mastered the four requirements necessary to become a Scout, you will be invested as a Scout. Your parents or guardians and other members of your family may be invited to your investiture ceremony.

During the ceremony, which you may share with one or two other new Scouts, the Troop Scouter will ask you to make the Scout Promise in front of your fellow Scouts. Your Scouter will also remind you of the seven parts of the Scout Law, which you will use to guide your actions both as a Scout and in life, in general.

At the end of the ceremony, your Scouter will present you with Scout epaulettes (tan uniform) or the Scout pin (t-shirt option) — your identification as a member of a worldwide brotherhood of Scouts. You will also receive a number of other badges that show you belong to a particular patrol, Scout group, district or area, and province. You will also get your neckerchief. Some Scout troops wear the Canadian Scout neckerchief.
It's navy blue with a gold maple leaf on the point.
Other troops wear neckerchiefs of a design and colour that represent their particular group. In such cases, Wolf Cubs, Venturers, and Rovers who also belong to that group wear the same neckerchief.

Congratulations. You're now a Scout!

I was invested in the ———————— Troop
on ———— by Scouter————————————

DID YOU KNOW IN 1997, SCOUTING CELEBRATED ITS 90TH ANNIVERSARY, and CJ'97 was held in Thunder Bay, Ontario? About 11,500 attended.

WHAT'S NEXT

Now that you are invested, you will want to continue on with the fun and adventure of Scouting.

LINK BADGE

When you're invested as a Scout, you may be eligible to receive a Link Badge. If you were a member of a Wolf Cub pack before you joined your Scout troop, then you should have worked on the requirements for a Link Badge. These requirements make up most of the Scout investiture requirements. The badge's two colours (yellow and green) stand for Wolf Cubs and Scouts.

If you were a Beaver before you were a Cub, you would have received a brown and yellow Link Badge at your Cub investiture. You can continue to wear that Link Badge as a Scout.

Cub to Scout Link Badge requirements.

a) has been a registered Cub;

b) knows and understands the Scout Promise, Law and Motto; and

c) has taken part in at least three Scout activities.

Another Link Badge (this one green and blue) awaits you when you join a Venturer company.

Scout to Venturer Link Badge requirements.

a) has been a registered Scout;

b) knows and understands the Venturer Promise, Law and Motto; and

c) has taken part in at least three Venturer activities.

Cub Activity Awards

As the holder of any or all of the "Cub Activity Awards", you are permitted to transfer them to your Scout sash (see Uniform page for correct placement). When the equivalent Scout badge, as shown in the chart below, is earned, the Cub Activity Award is replaced.

Scout Badge	Cub Badge
Voyageur level - Outdoor Skills ➡ Remove (any or all)	- Canadian Camper Award - Canadian Heritage Trails Award - Canadian Wilderness Award
Voyageur level - Personal Development ➡ Remove (any or all)	- Canadian Arts Award - Canadian Healthy Living Award
Voyageur level - Citizenship ➡ Remove	- World Citizen Award
Voyageur level - Leadership ➡ Remove	- Canadian Family Care Award - Emergency Preparedness Award

KIM

Kim is the shortened form of the name Kimball O'Hara. In a book called Kim, written by Rudyard Kipling, Kim is an orphaned Irish boy brought up in India during the 19th century. In the book, Kim becomes a master of disguise and observation.

Perhaps you have played "Kim's Game." It comes from an episode in the book where Kim learns to develop his skills of observation. A jewelry dealer named Lurgan showed Kim a tray filled with precious jewels. Lurgan let Kim look for one minute and then covered the tray. Kim then had to tell Lurgan how many jewels were on the tray and what kind they were.

Kim is also the name given to a Scout who is part of the leadership team of a Wolf Cub Pack. Wolf Cubs are 8 to 10 years old. As a Kim, you will help with such things as games, crafts and stories. Though there will be times when you may do things with all the Cubs, you will probably be more involved with the older Cubs who will soon be Scouts. When you perform your duties as Kim with the Cub Pack, you wear a special yellow neckerchief with a Kim badge on the back. Normally, a Kim is a Scout who has completed at least one year in the Scout program. If you think you might like to be a Kim, speak to your Patrol Counsellor. He will put you in touch with Wolf Cub Pack leaders who will be able to explain the job to you. You might also like to look at The Kim Book, which will tell you more about the duties of a Kim. The book also explains how you can combine being a Kim with working on some of your Scout badge requirements.

I was a Kim with the_____ Pack
from _____ to _____

THE SCOUT SYMBOL

As Scouting's emblem, B.-P. chose the sign for the
North Point which is "universally shown on maps,
charts and compass cards" because "it points in the
right direction (and upwards), turning neither to the
right nor left, since they lead backward again..." Lady
Baden-Powell later added the further explanation, "It
shows the true way to go."

But how did the sign for the North Point get to be
a fleur-de-lis (pronounced flur-de-lee)? According
to B.-P., in the Middle Ages, mariner Flavio Gioja
made the seaman's compass into a more practical
and reliable instrument. In Italian, "north" was
"tramontana." Gioja used the capital "T" on the
compass card, but to show respect to King Charles
of Naples whose crest was the fleur-de-lis, Gioja
combined the letter with that emblem.
Fittingly, the fleur-de-lis is also a
symbol of peace and purity.

To explain further the meaning of
the Scout emblem, B.-P. said, "The
two stars on the two side arms
stand for the two eyes of the Wolf
Cub having been opened before he
became a Scout..." The three points
of the fleur-de-lis, remind the Scout of the
three parts of the Scout's Promise: duty to God,

obedience to the Scout Law, and service to others."
The ring holding the emblem together represents
the bond of brotherhood among Scouts all over
the world.

THE WORLD SCOUT EMBLEM

Did you know that Scouting goes from A to Z? That's
right. Scouting is found around the world in more
than 217 countries and territories from Algeria to
Zimbabwe. One badge that each of the
25 million Scout members around
the world can wear is the World
Scout Emblem. When you buy
your Scout uniform, the World
Scout Emblem will be on it; it's
stitched into the left side above
the pocket.

The World Scout Emblem has two parts: a fleur-
de-lis, and a circle of rope tied with a reef knot. The
fleur-de-lis represents the Scouting Movement. The
rope circle, joined with a reef knot, symbolizes the
strength and unity of the world brotherhood of
Scouting. Why do you think Baden-Powell selected
the reef knot to join together the two ends
of the rope?

DID YOU KNOW THE SCOUT SYMBOL was chosen
by B.-P. as it signifies the sign for the North Point on a
map. Thus "it shows the true way to go."

The emblem is white on a royal purple background. Baden-Powell chose these colours because in heraldry, white stands for purity and purple for leadership and helping others.

Since Scouting began in 1908, over 200 million Scouts have worn the Scout symbol.

THE MAN WHO STARTED SCOUTING

Robert Baden-Powell, the man who started the Scouting Movement, spent over 30 years as an officer in the British army. It was while he was soldiering that he began to develop a number of ideas about how soldiers — especially military scouts — should be trained.

B.-P. (as we fondly call him) was a soldier before there were aircraft to spot enemy locations and strengths. In his time, if an army wanted to know what the enemy was doing, it had to send out military scouts to do a reconnaissance. B.-P. thought that such scouts would be more effective if they were self-reliant. To encourage his military scouts to develop this self-reliance, B.-P. organized them into small groups with their own leader. His ideas were published in an army booklet called *Aids to Scouting*.

Around the turn of the century, Baden-Powell received worldwide attention when he commanded a force of soldiers that defended the town of Mafeking in South Africa. For 217 days, Baden-Powell's forces resisted the efforts of a larger Boer force to dislodge them. Needing to stretch his manpower, B.-P. organized a cadet corps of local boys to serve as messengers, first aiders, and lookouts, and to do other useful tasks so

the soldiers could concentrate on defending the town. Finally, another British force arrived to lift the siege. B.-P. returned to England as a hero.

In 1904, B.-P. was asked to attend the annual inspection of the Boy's Brigade. After the event, B.-P. told the Brigade's founder, Sir William Smith, that he thought the Brigade would have a larger membership if its program were more varied and less based on the army's military drill. He offered some suggestions, and Smith proposed that B.-P. write a book for boys similar to *Aids to Scouting*.

Four years passed before the book appeared. During that time, B.-P. did the necessary research, and talked to others involved with youth organizations. Before he began to write, he decided to test out his ideas.

In 1907, he took 21 boys between the ages of 11 and 16 to Brownsea Island off the southern coast of England. There, he organized them into patrols and taught them some basic self-reliance skills. During the week, they pitched tents, swam, cooked meals outdoors, and learned to track, and tie knots. In short, they "scouted."

When it was first published, B.-P.'s book didn't appear as a whole book. Instead, it came out in six parts. The first installment of *Scouting for Boys* appeared on Wednesday, January 15, 1908. It was an immediate success, and boys (and girls, too) eagerly awaited every other Wednesday until the end of March 1908 for the new sections to arrive.

When B.-P. wrote *Scouting for Boys*, he didn't intend to start another organization, and he really didn't. Boys did, because Scout patrols and Scout troops began to spring up entirely on their own all over the country. By 1909, there were already about 100,0000 Scouts.

In 1910, the King of England (Edward VII) asked Baden-

Powell to resign from the army and devote himself full time to the Scouting Movement.

Scouting has continued to grow, and now there are more than 28 million members in 216 countries and territories around the globe. It's not known exactly which troop was the first in Canada. When B.-P. visited our country in August 1910, he per-suaded the Governor General, Earl Grey, to become Chief Scout of Canada.

On June 12, 1914, the Boy Scouts of Canada were incorporated by an Act of Parliament.

B.-P. had an exciting childhood, and some of his exploits and adventures as a soldier and spy were absolutely thrilling. If you want to read more about B.-P.'s life, check your school or public library for *B.-P.'s Life in Pictures*, or *Baden-Powell: The Man Who Lived Twice*, by Mary Drewery. Another book to look at is Baden-Powell's *Scouting for Boys*. Ask your Patrol Counsellor if the troop owns any of these books.

Lord Robert Stephenson Smyth Baden-Powell of Gilwell was born on February 22, 1857, in London, England, and died on January 8, 1941, in Kenya. Every year, the week in February that contains B.-P.'s birth date is called **Scout-Guide Week**. Your patrol or troop will probably want to do something special during that week as a way of remembering this man whose imagination provided the spark for the worldwide brotherhood of Scouting.

B.-P. THE ARTIST

If Baden-Powell had been a Scout rather than the founder of Scouting, his first Challenge Badge probably would have been Artist. Originally, Baden-Powell was a military officer; one time he used his drawing interest and ability to fool an enemy. He disguised himself as a butterfly collector and went close to the enemy's fortifications. There he made drawings of "butterflies." Actually, hidden inside the butterflies' markings were the locations of the enemy's weapons.

When enemy soldiers challenged Baden-Powell, all they could see in his drawings were the butterflies. By looking at the two pictures, you can see how he hid the information he needed in the butterflies' wings.

If you want to know more about other exciting episodes in Baden-Powell's life, read *B.-P.'s Life in Pictures*. Your Patrol Counsellor can tell you how to get a copy. Perhaps your Counsellor has the book *Scouting for Boys*, by Baden-Powell. It includes more of his sketches.

OUTLINE OF A FORT IN A SKETCH OF A BUTTERFLY

This sketch of a butterfly contains the outline of a fortress, and marks both the position and the power of the fort's guns. The marks on the wings between the lines mean nothing, but those on the lines show the nature and the size of the guns, according to the key. The position of each gun is at the place inside the outline of the fort on the butterfly where the line marked with the spot ends.

Key: The marks on the wings reveal the shape of the fortress shown here, and the size of the guns.

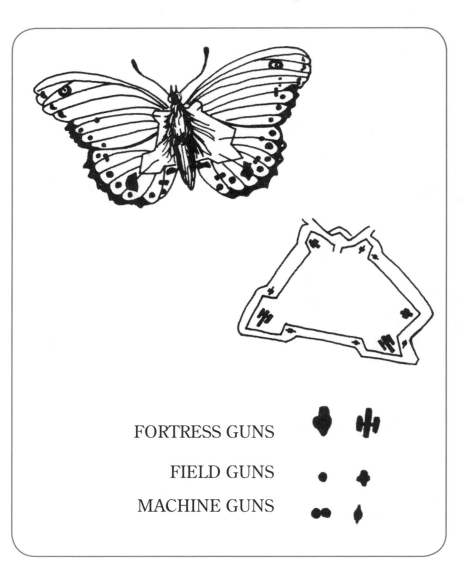

FORTRESS GUNS

FIELD GUNS

MACHINE GUNS

ACTIVITY BADGES

If you have looked through the rest of this book, you may have noticed that there are two types of badges Scouts can earn and wear. Some have a round shape while others are diamond shaped and have different coloured borders.

The round badges are called Challenge Badges. We'll discuss them later.

The diamond badges are called Activity Badges. Their coloured borders — brown or green — tell what level of each badge you have earned. You wear both levels of the badges on your sash.

The Activity Badges are connected to the three achievement awards: Voyageur Scout Award, Pathfinder Scout Award, and the Chief Scout's Award. As the chart on page 62-63 shows, to earn each Award, you must earn all Activity Badges, as well as a certain number of Challenge Badges.

Normally you will progress through the two levels of each Activity Badge from brown to green. But there are some exceptions. Some Activity Badge requirements are connected to activities you might be doing outside Scouting. First Aid and Lifesaving are two such examples. Here, you may already have accomplished certain requirements.

You may already hold certificates or badges from the St. John Ambulance Association (for first aid), the Lifesaving Society of Canada (for water rescue), or the Canadian Red Cross or the YMCA (for swimming). If you hold any appropriate awards from these other agencies, and there is a corresponding badge, you will receive the equivalent Scout badge.

Whenever possible, it's a good idea for patrol members to work together on the requirements of an Activity Badge. Some badges, in fact, call for you to do things with your patrol. For example, the Voyageur level of the Outdoor Skills Activity Badge asks you to "participate in two hikes/outings of approximately 6 hours duration each" with members of your patrol. Use a patrol meeting to decide what activities you will do in order to meet the requirements of badges your patrol will work on.

As you progress, you will find you're expected to share your new knowledge and skills with Scouts who are working at a lower level of the badges.

For example, Scouts working on the Pathfinder Leadership Activity Badge are asked to "teach a basic level skill to a Scout working at the Pioneer or Voyageur level." This requirement lets you pass along your knowledge of such things as camp cooking or the use of camp stoves or lanterns to less experienced Scouts.

Now let's take a closer look at how the Activity Badges are connected to the Voyageur and Pathfinder Awards.

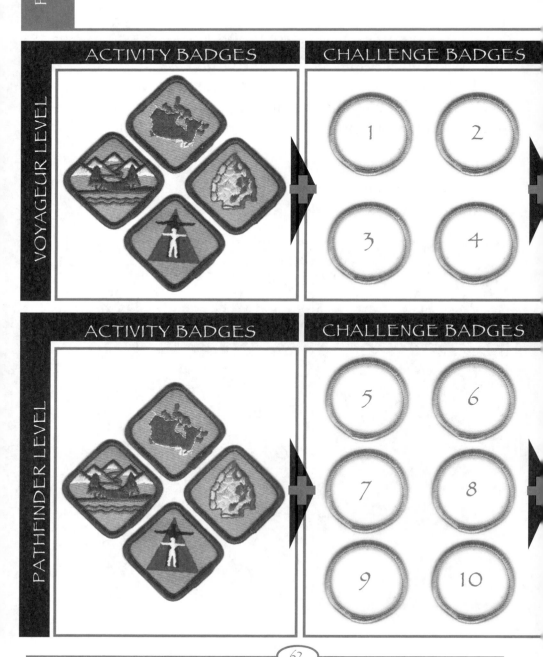

PIONEER LEVEL

Complete the Investitiure Requirements to become a Pioneer Scout

VOYAGEUR LEVEL

ACTIVITY BADGES

CHALLENGE BADGES

1 2
3 4

PATHFINDER LEVEL

ACTIVITY BADGES

CHALLENGE BADGES

5 6
7 8
9 10

ACHIEVES

 or

SCOUT EPAULETTES

YEAR ROUND CAMPER	ACHIEVES

VOYAGEUR LEVEL

**VOYAGEUR
SCOUT AWARD**

YEAR ROUND CAMPER	ACHIEVES

PATHFINDER LEVEL

**PATHFINDER
SCOUT AWARD**

63

PIONEERS

Although Canada's first true pioneers were the original peoples who lived in this land, we usually apply the term to those who followed the European explorers and settled in Canada. The men and women who came to Canada as pioneers could not bring many possessions with them. Because they had no stores or mail-order catalogues where they could buy the things they wanted or needed, pioneers had to be as self-sufficient and self-reliant as possible.

Pioneers had to learn to make many of the things they needed. To survive, they needed to have some basics, such as food, shelter, clothing, furniture and fuel. That meant, for example, they had to know which wood types were good for fires or for building homes or for making furniture.

Cooperation among pioneers was also very important for their survival. Pioneer families often got together to help each other build houses and barns, clear fields for planting, and harvest crops.

In what ways might you and your patrol be like pioneers?

PIONEER SCOUT

Know and understand:

☐ Scout Promise

☐ Scout Law

Know and understand:

☐ Scout Motto

☐ Scout Slogan

Know and understand:

☐ Scout Handshake

☐ Scout Salute and Sign

☐ The reasons Scouts use them

☐ Participate in one Scout troop activity (preferably outdoors)

Troop Activity _____

_____

Upon completion of the above, the youth is invested as a Pioneer Scout.

*Youth members of the troop (preferably the patrol leaders) are to conduct the training and testing of these requirements.

Photo of the ceremony

Here's me becoming a **Pioneer Scout**.

VOYAGEUR

Voyageur was a term given in the 17th and 18th centuries to the adventurous men who journeyed long distances by canoe from Montreal to western and northern Canada to trade for furs. It was a very demanding life. To be a voyageur, you had to have good canoeing skills and be able to paddle long distances. A good voyageur paddled 40 strokes a minute from dawn to dusk. You also had to be strong, because rapids and waterfalls meant sometimes portaging your canoe and its load long distances over rough ground. And you had to be able to camp and cook using local foods.

The large fur canoes, called Montreal Canoes, were about 11 metres long, two metres wide, and needed a crew of six to twelve voyageurs. The smaller North Canoe was eight metres long, and over a metre wide. It carried a crew of four to eight voyageurs. Everyone on the crew had to work as part of a team to paddle and portage the canoe, and each voyageur had to do his job. Sometimes as they paddled, the voyageurs sang songs to keep up their spirits and help them maintain their paddling rhythm.

How was a North Canoe and its crew of voyageurs like you and your patrol?

VOYAGEUR AWARD REQUIREMENTS

1. Pioneer Scout

2. At the Voyageur level, complete:
   Citizenship ——————date completed
   Leadership ——————date completed
   Personal Development——————date completed
   Outdoor Skills ——————date completed

3. Four Challenge Badges from at least two categories.
   Badge 1. ——————2. ——————
          3. ——————4. ——————

   Category 1. ——————2. ——————

4. Spring/Fall portion of Year-Round Camper Award
   Spring/Fall ——————date completed

Completion of the above earns the VOYAGEUR AWARD.

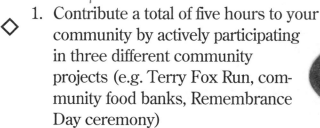

Citizenship

◇ 1. Contribute a total of five hours to your community by actively participating in three different community projects (e.g. Terry Fox Run, community food banks, Remembrance Day ceremony)

◇ 2. Describe what to do at the scene of an emergency, including how to report fires, accidents or crimes using the "911" service, or other emergency service used in your community.

◇ 3. Demonstrate a knowledge of your community by being able to give simple directions (e.g. how to get to major features of the community such as a police station, a hospital, a shopping centre, or a sports facility).

◇ 4. Meet with a representative of a local public service (fire department, police service, ambulance service, engineering department) to learn its function and role within the community.

◇ 5. Describe the Canadian flag, as well as your provincial or territorial flag, flower and bird using visual aids to assist.

◇ 6. Demonstrate the correct care and use of the Canadian Flag while participating in a flag ceremony.

◇ 7. Research the National War Memorial located in Ottawa, and explain its significance to your Patrol/Troop. Identify any contributions made by your relatives toward Canada's protection of peace and freedom in the world.

◇ 8. Creatively demonstrate your knowledge of the history of Scouting, as described in the Canadian Scout Handbook (pages 48-56).

I got my **Citizenship Badge** on
(Date) _____

Leadership —

◇ 1. Show your ability to be a contributing member of a group by planning and participating in a patrol/ troop activity which meets a requirement of the Voyageur level – OUTDOOR SKILLS.

◇ 2. Discuss the difference between a "boss" and a "leader" with your Court of Honour, or Patrol in Council. Provide examples of each style through role-play with your patrol members.

◇ 3. Select a person who has a leadership role in your community and discuss and evaluate their methods. In your own words, explain what makes this person a good leader. Examples of this person might include coaches, Scout leaders, teachers and service club members.

◇ 4. Describe the roles and responsibilities of the patrol leader, assistant patrol leader, activity leader, and Scout leader.

◇ 5. Help plan a skills or activity session for the troop, and evaluate how the session went.

◇ 6. Discuss the function and purpose of the Court of Honour, and patrol meeting.

◇ 7. Develop and practise a home fire plan with your family. Discuss the successes, and identify the shortcomings of your plan.

I got my **Leadership Badge** on
(Date) _____

Personal Development — Spiritual

◇ 1. Lead your troop in a spiritual activity such as a reading, prayer, or grace.

◇ 2. Participate in the planning and conducting of a Scout's Own.

◇ 3. Attend a faith service of your choice, or participate in a Scout's Own with your troop.

Social

◇ 4. Record ways that you have used the Scout Promise and Law in your daily living.

◇ 5. Discuss with your parents, Section II of *"How to Protect Your Children from Child Abuse."*

◇ 6. Discuss the effects of peer pressure. Describe how peer pressure affects you.

◇ 7. Participate in a discussion of the effects of alcohol, tobacco, and drugs.

Intellectual

◇ 8. Explain the importance of goal-setting.

◇ 9. Demonstrate setting personal goals, including the steps that will be required in order to achieve your goal.

◇ 10. Discuss your goals with your Scout leader and family.

Physical

◇ 11. Show that you understand the following aspects of personal health and hygiene as they pertain to a camping environment:

    a) Care of skin, hair and nails;

    b) Care of eyes, ears and teeth;

    c) Proper amount of sleep;

    d) Functions of the main organs of the body; and

    e) Care of allergies.

◇ 12. Understand general public health measures, which include water treatment and immunization.

◇ 13. Explain the value of exercise.

◇ 14. Participate and show ability in an individual or team sport.

◇ 15. Demonstrate basic fitness level in five different exercise areas:

  a) Push-ups (5);

  b) Shuttle run (14 second); (3 shuttles, 10 metres from start)

  c) Partial curl-ups (17);

  d) Standing long jump (1.35 m);

  e) 50 m run (10 sec.); and

  f) Endurance run (1600 metres 10 min, 15 sec).

OR

◇ 16. Show successful participation in an appropriate physical fitness program.

I got my **Personal Development Badge** on (Date) _____

Outdoor Skills —

With members of your patrol and/or troop, participate in the following outdoor activities:

◇ 1. Camp outdoors for a minimum of six (6) nights. (Two nights must be consecutive.)

◇ 2. Participate in two (2) hikes/outings of approximately 6 hours duration each — one may be included in the camps detailed above. One hike or outing must involve an overnight stay in the outdoors.

◇ 3. Demonstrate your knowledge of weather conditions and the hazards that can be encountered including knowledge of the causes, symptoms, signs, prevention and treatment of the following:

- hypothermia;
- hyperthermia;
- frostbite;
- sunburn/sunstroke; and
- dehydration.

◇ 4. Prepare a list of basic personal equipment you need for an overnight camp. Know about its uses and maintenance.

◇ 5. Discuss the rules and procedures your troop uses to prevent getting lost or separated from the group. Describe what you would do if you

◇ became lost or separated from your patrol.

6. Prepare a personal emergency kit. Describe
◇ the contents and purpose of each item.

7. Demonstrate your knowledge of environmental conditions, and the hazards that can be encountered in the outdoors by:

   a) Describing the dangers of severe storms and how to protect yourself during a lightning or hail storm or tornado, etc.;

   b) Describing how to deal with biting and stinging insects when outdoors (e.g. What colours attract insects? What clothing should you wear? How do you handle allergic reactions?);

   c) Describing what dangers can be encountered from wild animals when outdoors. Give examples how you can minimize dangerous encounters (e.g. How would you react in the presence of a mother bear and her cub?); and

d) Researching what poisonous wild plants may be encountered in areas where your patrol camps. Describe the first aid treatment for one of them.

8. Demonstrate the safe use of your troop equipment (e.g. knives, axes, saws, stoves and lanterns).

9. Demonstrate your knowledge of maps (both road and topographical) and compass:

a) Know the 16 points of a compass and their corresponding degrees;

b) Know basic map symbols; and

c) Know how to take and follow compass bearings.

◇ 10. After exploring the potential impact of outdoor activities on the environment, develop your own "Environmental Code." Share your ideas with your patrol/troop.

◇ 11. Participate for at least a day in an environmental project of your choosing.

◇ 12. Demonstrate the ability to lay, light and safely extinguish a fire leaving no trace.

◇ 13. Cook a simple outdoor meal.

◇ 14. Demonstrate how to ensure safe drinking water.

◇ 15. Demonstrate safe campsite layout, paying particular interest to fuel, equipment and food storage, and fire safety.

◇ 16. Demonstrate the ability to use five common knots, and describe their correct use. (Knots to consider include: reef knot, locking bowline, clove hitch, sheetbend, round turn and two half hitches, and woven figure 8 bend.)

◇ 17. Demonstrate knowledge of Leave No Trace philosophies.

I got my **Outdoor Skills Badge** on
(Date) _____

Photo of the ceremony

Here's me getting my **Voyageur Scout Award**.

PATHFINDERS

Pathfinders are explorers who find new paths. Using their skill and courage, they travel into previously unexplored areas and mark out routes so others may follow. Canada's first pathfinders were this land's original people. Unfortunately, their names were not recorded. Instead, when we talk about Canada's pathfinders, we often use the names of European explorers like Pierre Radisson and Médard Groseilliers, Pierre de la Verendrye, Alexander Mackenzie, Henry Kelsey, David Thompson, Henry Hudson, Anthony Henday, and Samuel Hearne.

Perhaps you think pathfinders are just people of the past. But you can be a pathfinder in today's world; simply go where no man or woman has gone before. Where you go might even be out of this world, like Canada's first astronaut, Commander Marc Garneau. Or you could be a pathfinder like mountaineer Jim Elzinga, one of only four Canadians ever to climb Mount Everest, the world's highest mountain. Other pathfinders don't go anywhere but, like Alexander Graham Bell, they invent things such as the telephone. Who knows, you might become another Jonas Salk and discover a vaccine that will prevent a harmful disease like polio.

There are limitless opportunities for becoming a pathfinder. What kind of pathfinder will you be?

PATHFINDER AWARD REQUIREMENTS

◇ 1. Voyageur Scout

◇ 2. At the Pathfinder level, complete:
Citizenship ——————date completed
Leadership ——————date completed
Personal Development——————date completed
Outdoor Skills ——————date completed

◇ 3. Six more Challenge Badges from at least
2 new categories.
Badge   1. —————— 2.——————
           3. —————— 4.——————
           5. —————— 6.——————

Category 1. —————— 2.——————

◇ 4. Summer and Winter portion of Year-Round
Camper Award.
Summer ——————date completed
Winter ——————date completed

Completion of the above earns the
PATHFINDER AWARD.

Citizenship —

◇ 1. Identify the following flags: the United Nations, World Scout, Canadian provinces and territories.

◇ 2. With other members of your patrol, meet with a member of local government or the legal system. Discuss with this person their responsibilities and the workings of their system.

◇ 3. Explain the following to show that you understand how the Government of Canada works: the roles of the Queen, Governor General, and Lieutenant Governors; the general functions or powers of federal, provincial and local governments; the role of civil servants and the role of political parties.

◇ 4. Meet with a member of a local service club, and discuss their organization's role in the community.

◇ 5. Know how to do the following in your community:

    a) Report damage or need for repairs to roads and bridges;

    b) Report damage to electrical power, sewer mains, water supply systems;

    c) Report a hazardous materials spill;

d) Obtain a building permit for a house or garage; and

e) Report suspected water contamination to the local health authority.

◇ 6. With members of your patrol, visit a historic memorial site and explain its significance to the community.

OR

◇ Visit an industrial plant, business or educational centre. During your visit, find out about the types of jobs or careers that are available.

OR

◇ Report on the history, growth and present role of one of the following: Royal Canadian Mounted Police, Canadian Armed Forces, Supreme Court of Canada.

◇ 7. Actively participate in five community projects. At least two must be different from the choices made at the Voyageur level.

◇ 8. Communicate and explore local Scouting activities with a Scout from another area or culture. (This could be done in person, or by letter, fax, ham radio, or e-mail.)

I got my **Citizenship Pathfinder Badge** on (Date) _____

Leadership —

◇ 1. Research a local or world leader. Lead a ten-minute discussion about this leader (including the leadership role he or she played) in your patrol or troop.

◇ 2. Plan and participate in leading an all-day outdoor activity for your patrol. Evaluate the event with your patrol at the end of the activity.

◇ 3. Using a patrol meeting, plan and conduct a troop camping trip lasting at least forty-eight hours. A detailed plan will be developed showing the steps necessary to have a successful venture. Evaluate the event with your patrol at the end of the activity.

◇ 4. Teach a basic level skill to a Scout working at the Pioneer or Voyageur level skills. At the end of your activity the Scout must successfully demonstrate good knowledge of the subject.

◇ 5. Provide a leadership role to another group (Cubs, church, sports, etc.). Discuss your experience with your patrol leader and/or Scouter.

I got my **Leadership Pathfinder Badge** on (Date) _____

Personal Development —
Spiritual

◇ 1. Understand the role of your religion, spiritual belief, and/or church. Discuss your beliefs with the spiritual advisor of your choice. (Requirement satisfied by Green Religion in Life award.)

◇ 2. Prepare and perform a leading role in a Scout's Own.

Social

◇ 3. Explore the area of social interaction with others. Subjects may include: dating, behaviour in public, sexually transmitted diseases, and abusive behaviours.

◇ 4. Know and demonstrate good personal grooming habits.

◇ 5. Explore at least two issues of public health. Subjects may include: AIDS, contagious diseases, blood supply, or Medicare.

◇ 6. Explore at least two issues of public safety and security. Subjects may include: Neighbourhood Watch, Block Parents, swarming, public facility safety, or safety inspectors.

◇ 7. Research and report on the effects of alcohol, tobacco and drugs.

Intellectual

◇ 8. Review your goals made for the Voyageur level and:

    a) evaluate your progress towards goals set in the Voyageur level; and

    b) set new goals based on your progress in the Voyageur level.

Physical

◇ 9. Demonstrate knowledge of emergency treatment and first aid by qualifying at the St. John's "Emergency First Aid" level, or the Red Cross "Emergency level",

OR

◇ 10. By demonstration, discussion or participation,

show good knowledge of the following:

    a) How to treat shock and choking;

    b) Demonstrate not less than five (5) bandaging techniques using triangular bandages. (Scouts must demonstrate at least one method of stabilizing fractures.)

    c) The meaning of first aid, and the management of a case;

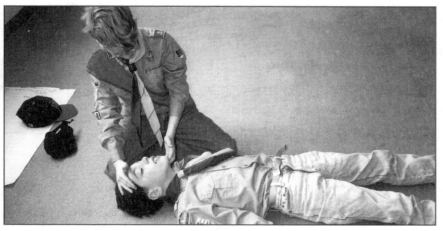

d) The types of wounds, and dangers of infections;

e) The general rules for treating fractures and poisons, as well as bleeding wounds;

f) How to control bleeding;

g) How to make a stretcher and splints from items found at the site of an accident;

h) How to treat an arm for a cut, burn and scald; and

i) CPR

Note: A qualified instructor must deliver the training.

I got my **Personal Development Pathfinder Badge** by _____ on
(Date) _____

Outdoor Skills —

With members of your patrol and/ or troop, participate in the following outdoor activities and demonstrate advanced skills and abilities. Be able to use equipment with little or no supervision.

◇ 1. Camp outdoors for a minimum of six (6) nights, not including those done for the Voyageur Award. This must include at least two, two-night or one, three-night camps, and one lightweight or mobile camp.

◇ 2. Participate in three (3) additional hikes/ trips of at least six (6) hours duration each.

   a) One must include an overnight stay of at least two nights. (These nights may be included in the camps detailed above).

   b) Another must be during winter conditions.

Note: For the purpose of this requirement, alternate methods may be chosen (e.g. bikes, cross-country skiing, horseback riding, canoeing, etc). Motorized transportation is not acceptable.

◇ 3. Demonstrate the proper care, use and maintenance of equipment, including stoves, tents, axes, saws, and cooking equipment.

◇ 4. Plan a menu for two Scouts for a weekend camp.

    a) The plan shall have a minimum of five (5) meals.

    b) The plan must include a food and supplies list, which includes quantity.

◇ 5. Plan a balanced menu for a patrol of Scouts for a weekend camp. The plan shall have a minimum of five (5) meals, and must include a food and supplies list which details quantities required.

◇ 6. Sleep overnight in a temporary shelter that you built, while minimizing the damage to the environment.

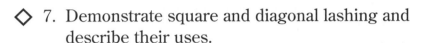

◇ 7. Demonstrate square and diagonal lashing and describe their uses.

◇ 8. Demonstrate to Voyageur level Scouts the proper care, maintenance and packing of personal camping gear suitable for a two-day camp. Include sleeping bag, pack, clothes, boots, etc.

◇ 9. Identify four wild birds and four mammals that are indigenous to the area where you live or camp. Keep a list of the sightings you encounter on at least two camps or hikes.

◇ 10. Identify four types of trees/shrubs in the area you camp or hike.

◇ 11. Identify four types of wild flowers in the area you camp or hike.

◇ 12. Demonstrate the proper disposal of cooking residues, grey water, and body waste.

◇ 13. Plan and lead an environmental project for your patrol/troop.

◇ 14. Demonstrate throughout the Pathfinder Award that you have put into practice your personal Environmental Code and Leave No Trace philosophies.

I got my **Outdoor Skills Pathfinder Badge** by
_____ on
(Date) _____

Photo of the ceremony

Here's me getting my **Pathfinder Scout Award**.

The Chief Scout's Award was created in September 1973 by Governor General Roland Michener, who was then Chief Scout of Canada. You will receive the award when you complete the following requirements.

1. Successfully complete the Pathfinder Scout requirements.

2. Be currently qualified in First Aid Standard level or demonstrate the equivalent attitudes, skills and knowledge as judged by a "qualified instructor of First Aid".

3. Have earned at least one Challenge Badge in each of the seven (7) Challenge Badge Categories: Athletics, Outdoors, Science & Technology, Home & Family, Personal Development, Culture & Society, Environment.

4. Hold the World Conservation Badge.

5. Investigate Scouts Canada's involvement in World Scouting. Present your findings in an interesting way to your patrol, troop, or other group. Your presentation should include information on the following:

a) Scouts Canada's involvement with:
   - the Canadian Scout Brotherhood Fund;
   - world jamborees; and
   - the World Organization of the Scout Movement (WOSM).

b) The purpose and location of the World Scouting Bureau; and

c) The current World Scouting membership, and how Canada's membership compares to that of other countries.

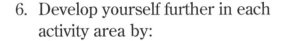

6. Develop yourself further in each activity area by:

a) Designing a challenging program with a Scouter which includes the requirement to excel in a component of each activity area (Citizenship, Leadership, Personal Development, and Outdoor Skills). Citizenship must include providing at least 30 hours of leadership to others.

These hours are in addition to the hours required for the Citzenship Activity Area. If at all possible, provide this service outside of Scouting

b) Offering your plans and goals for discussion, and approval to your Court of Honour and Troop Scouter prior to beginning.

c) Reporting to, and being evaluated by, the Court of Honour and Troop Scouter on your ongoing progress.

Requirement 3

These are the Challenge Badges in each category that I earned for my CHIEF SCOUT'S AWARD.

Athletics Category ———————————————

Outdoors Category ———————————————

Home & Family Category ——————————

Personal Development Category ——————

Science & Technology Category ——————

Culture & Society Category ————————

Environment Category ————————————

Requirement 6

My Challenging Program Outline

Citizenship Activity Area   # of hours
Description: ——————————————————

———————————————————————

Leadership Activity Area
Description: ——————————————————

———————————————————————

Personal Development Activity Area
Description: ——————————————————

———————————————————————

Outdoor Skills Activity Area
Description: ——————————————————

———————————————————————

The Chief Scout's Award will be yours when you have completed these six (6) requirements as judged by your fellow Scouts, the Troop Scouter and Patrol Counsellors. Generally, your Troop Scouter will

present you the emblem. A certificate signed by the
Chief Scout of Canada will be presented to you at
a public ceremony. You continue to wear the Chief
Scout's Award as a Venturer. If you have not completed
all of the requirements for the Chief Scout's Award
before you join a Venturer Company, you have three
months in which to complete them.

I received my **Chief Scout's Award**
on (Date) —————————— at a ceremony held at

——————————————————————————————————

Here's me getting my Chief Scout's Award.

Photo of the ceremony

Congratulations! You are now a holder of the Chief Scout's Award — the highest award in the Scout program. There is only one Chief Scout of Canada (the Governor General of Canada) just as there was only one Chief Scout of the World. He, of course, was Robert Baden-Powell, Scouting's founder.

* see note

1

Pathfinder
Scout Award
or
All equivalent
requirements

Choose one & enter

1.

Date completed
_____

Plus **3**

Category	Badge
Athletic	_____
Culture & Society	_____
Environment	_____
Home & Family	_____
Outdoors	_____
Personnal Development	_____
Science & Technology	_____

Date completed
_____

Plus **6**

Challenging program

Activity Area	Requirements
Citizenship	_____
Leadership	_____
Personnal Development	_____
Outdoor Skills	_____

*Note : Make sure a local commissioner reviews your path to the
Chief Scout's Award **before** you begin.

Plus **2**

Current
St. John's
Ambulance
or
Current
Canadian
Red Cross
or
Equivalent

First Aid
Standard
Level

Choose one & enter

1.

Date completed
_____

Plus **4**

World Conservation
Award

Date completed
_____

Plus **5**

World Scouting
Involvement

Date completed
_____

Date completed _____
Date completed _____
Date completed _____
Date completed _____

This certifies that
(name) _____
has completed all requirements
of the Chief Scout's Award,
to the satisfaction of the
Court of Honour

_____
signature

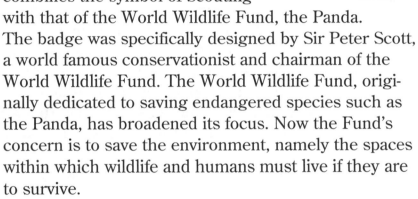

WORLD CONSERVATION AWARD

Purpose: To demonstrate a
Scout's concern for
the environment and
awareness of the global
need for conservation.

The World Conservation Badge
combines the symbol of Scouting
with that of the World Wildlife Fund, the Panda.
The badge was specifically designed by Sir Peter Scott,
a world famous conservationist and chairman of the
World Wildlife Fund. The World Wildlife Fund, originally dedicated to saving endangered species such as
the Panda, has broadened its focus. Now the Fund's
concern is to save the environment, namely the spaces
within which wildlife and humans must live if they are
to survive.

The World Conservation Badge is an international
badge, which means Scouts in other countries are also
working to earn it, even though they may be working
on slightly different requirements. All Scouts around
the world who wear this badge publicly demonstrate
Scouting's concern for the environment and awareness
of the global need for conservation.

To earn the World Conservation Badge (which you
wear on the back of the sash 3 cm from the top seam)
you must complete the following.

Requirements:

1. Complete at least two Challenge Badges in the environmental category;

2. Choose a conservation issue of importance to Canada and the world, and complete a project that includes some recognizable work in your community. Make a presentation, display or report describing your project, and the global importance of the issue in relation to Climate Change. You may complete the project as an individual or in a group. Examples might include global warming, acid rain, endangered species, etc.; and

3. Take a leading role in planning and conducting an environmental activity of your choice which focuses on the concept, "Think Globally, Act Locally."

The issue and project I/we chose to work on was

_____

I received my **World Conservation Award** on (Date) _____

CLIMATE CHANGE CHALLENGE
DÉFI CHANGEMENT CLIMATIQUE (See Page 213.)

YEAR-ROUND CAMPER AWARD

Purpose: This three-part award encourages you to get camping experience in different seasons of the year. As you camp just for fun or to complete the camping requirements for various badges, record your camping nights on the "Camping Checklist," page 110.

Camps: The three different types of camping are (i) summer, (ii) winter, and (iii) spring or fall. Because of the different climatic conditions across Canada, no specific calendar months are suggested for each season. Your Troop Scouter or Patrol Counsellor will determine the appropriate classification based on local weather conditions.

Requirements:
To qualify for the award:

1. You must spend at least two nights in each of the three camping periods in tents or other temporary shelter.

2. As a patrol, for each camp you must:

   a) Obtain written parental permission to camp;

b) Select the campsite and obtain permission to use it;

c) Arrange transportation. If you use a vehicle, you must travel the last kilometre on foot and carry in all your gear with your patrol members;

d) Develop a menu and buy the food you need;

e) Prepare the patrol camping equipment suitable for the season; and

f) Plan the program activities for the camp.

3. Get the approval of your Troop Scouter or Patrol Counsellor for all of your actions related to the items in #2.

4. Evaluate each camp with a Scouter within two weeks of the camp. Discuss your preparations, camp outcomes and Leave No Trace actions.

The Award: The award has three parts, each representing one of the three camping periods. There are no time restrictions on how long you may take to earn the Year-Round Camper Award. When you satisfactorily complete the requirements for a camping season, the appropriate section of the award will be presented to you.

Your patrol or troop may want to decide where you will wear the award. While you may wear it on the top of the back of your sash, you might also put it on your campfire blanket, a jacket, or even a camp hat. You may also want to decide whether you will sew on the sections as you earn them, or choose to wait until you've earned all the sections before wearing them.

As you complete the requirements for the award, ask your Troop Scouter or Patrol Counsellor to initial the appropriate part(s) of the checklist.

CHECKLIST	Spring/Fall		Winter		Summer	
	Night 1	2	Night 1	2	Night 1	2
Parental Permission						
Campsite Permission						
Transportation						
Menu						
Food Purchase						
Equipment						
Program						
Leader Approval						
Evaluation and Discussion						

I received my **Spring/Fall Camper Award**
from _____ on
(Date) _____

I received my **Summer Camper Award**
from _____ on
(Date) _____

I received my **Winter Camper Award**
from _____ on
(Date) _____

RELIGION IN LIFE AWARD

In making your Scout Promise, you said you will do your duty to God. How you personally demonstrate that can take many forms. One way might involve earning the Religion in Life emblem.

To help you earn this award, you need to get a pamphlet outlining the requirements for the faith of your choice from your Scout council office or Scouts Canada's web site, www.scouts.ca/inside.asp?cmpageid=276. Ask your Scout Counsellor or Troop Scouter to help you get it. Usually an adult from your faith will be appointed to help you with the requirements.

When you have completed the requirements, you will be presented with both an emblem and a certificate. Your Scout leader will probably arrange for a spiritual leader of your faith to present them to you at an appropriate occasion — perhaps at a religious service.

The Religion in Life Award has five stages. The emblem's outside border colour (yellow, green, blue, red, and purple — adults only) shows which stage you have earned. You may have earned the yellow stage as a Wolf Cub. If you did, you may continue to wear the emblem until you earn a higher level emblem as a Scout. You should only wear the highest stage you've earned. You wear the Religion in Life emblem on the right side of the sash at the top, just above the Link Badges and Language Strip.

There are eight different designs for the
Religion in Life emblem.

 The emblem of the Zoroastrian faith shows
a Fravashi, God's spark or essence in the form
of a guardian spirit. The symbol re-presents
the two worlds: the physical with the image of a man, and
the spiritual with the wings and tail of a bird.

 The emblem of the Jewish faith is the Meno-
rah, the Jewish symbol of light whose gentle
rays overcome darkness in the world.

 The emblem of the Christian faith is a great
circle, the symbol of eternity. In the circle are
the first and last letters of the Greek alphabet
— Alpha and Omega — the symbol of God Himself.

 The Dharma Cakra (Wheel of the Law) is the
Religion in Religion in Life emblem for the
Buddhist faith. It reveals the victorious wheel of
a thousand spokes, and represents the symmetry and com-
pleteness of the law.

 Hindus, are represented by OM,
the symbol of God.

 Although, there is no official Bahá'í emblem,
the nine-pointed star is often used as a sym
bol of the faith. Because nine is the highest
numerical digit, in Bahá'í it symbolizes com-
prehensiveness, culmination and perfection.

The Islamic Religion in Life emblem contains the word "Allah" in Arabic and English, and a crescent and star. "Allah" means God, while the crescent and star are established symbols of Islam.

 The Khanda is the Sikh symbol. The double-edge sword (also called a Khanda) is a metaphor of Divine Knowledge; its sharp edges cleave truth from falsehood. The circle around the Khanda symbolizes the perfection of God who is eternal. The two curved swords symbolize Temporal and Spiritual authority; a Sikh must emphasize these equally in life.

I received my **Religion in Life Award**,
yellow stage, from _____
on (date) _____
green stage, from _____
on (date) _____
blue stage, from _____
on (date) _____
red stage, from _____
on (date) _____

SPRITUALITY AWARD

 The Spirituality Award is designed for the youth member who is presently excluded from earning a religion-in-Life Award by not belonging to a specific faith community. To help you earn this award, obtain the pamphlet outlining the requirements from Scouts Canada's website.

I received my **Spirituality Award**
from _____ on
(Date) _____

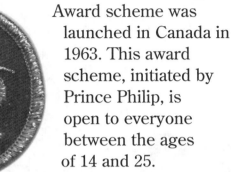

The Duke of Edinburgh's Award scheme was launched in Canada in 1963. This award scheme, initiated by Prince Philip, is open to everyone between the ages of 14 and 25.

The Duke of Edinburgh's Award scheme has three levels: Bronze, Silver, and Gold. The three levels are geared to different age groups — bronze for those over 14 years, silver for those over 15, and gold for those over 16.

The program has four sections: Service, Physical Fitness, Skills and Expeditions, and Explorations. Officials from different levels of government make the award presentations. A member of the Royal Family (sometimes Prince Philip himself) presents the Duke of Edinburgh's Gold Award.

If you're coming up to your 14th birthday and think you might be interested in the Duke of Edinburgh's Award scheme, visit their web site at www.theaward.org.

BEING PREPARED!

Probably no one sets out to be a hero and win a medal, but Scouting's motto is "Be Prepared." By using the skills you have learned as a Scout, you may save someone's life. Below are the citations read when Scouts were presented medals by the Governor General of Canada, who is also Canada's Chief Scout.

Scout Colin Puetz, 12, of Rose Valley, Saskatchewan, received the Silver Cross for gallantry with considerable risk. When his brother Jason, 2, was attacked by the family dog, Colin took quick and courageous action to save the badly mauled youngster from further injury or death. The Scout crawled under the patio on his stomach and elbows, moved slowly towards the child and dog, grabbed his little brother, and dragged him to safety.

Scout Craig Pool, 11, of Fergus, Ontario, received the Silver Cross for going to the rescue of Gordon Noel. Gordon had broken through ice into deep water of the Grand River. By carefully working his way onto the ice, Craig was able to pull Gordon to safety.

Through determined and persistent action, Scout Kendall Isnor, 13, of Wolfville, Nova Scotia, saved the life of 13-year-old Paul Fairclough, a non-swimmer, who had fallen into the turbulent waters of the Mersey River. Hearing Paul's cry, Kendall plunged into the river after him. As the frightened victim struggled, sometimes pulling Kendall under, the Scout applied all his lifesaving skills. Finally Kendall grasped Paul in a rescue hold, and swam safely to shore with him. For his action, Kendall was awarded the Silver Cross.

Wakened by a fire in the house, Scout Barkley Skeates-Hill, 13, of Warner, Alberta, roused 11 sleeping people and probably saved their lives. After alerting his parents upstairs, he returned to the basement to help seven children, including a 3-year-old, escape. For his actions, Barkley was awarded the Bronze Cross.

Scout Douglas Pettigrew of Devon, Alberta, rescued his 6-year-old brother when he fell into a fast-flowing creek. Drawing on his knowledge and skill, Douglas crouched down beside the creek, waited until his brother surfaced, and grabbed him by the arms to pull him to safety. His quick action saved his brother's life, and Douglas was awarded the Medal for Meritorious Conduct.

Scout Ty Hansen of Truro, Nova Scotia, heard cries for help from Robbie Yuill who, while walking along a dike, lost his footing and fell into deep water. Although injured during the process, Ty persisted in his efforts, pulled Robbie out of the water, and comforted him until he got him safely home. Ty's prompt action and skillful response saved Robbie's life. Ty was awarded the medal for Meritorious Conduct.

Scout G. Simeon Stairs, 11, of Hemmingford, Quebec, received the Medal for Meritorious Conduct for quick action that saved the life of his father, who had been seriously gored by a bull on their farm. Simeon manoeuvred his own tractor between the bull and his father, helped his father onto the tractor, and despite the risk of further attack, moved to a safe area and summoned first aid.

Scout Trevor James Wallworth of Dartmouth, Nova Scotia, with another life guard, saved a boy who was in danger of drowning after falling from a raft on Paper Mill Lake. Trevor located the boy, administered mouth to mouth resuscitation, and stayed with him until an ambulance arrived. He was awarded the Medal for Meritorious Conduct.

The Gold Cross
For Gallantry, with
special heroism and
extraordinary risk.

The Silver Cross
For Gallantry, with
considerable risk.

The Bronze Cross
For Gallantry, with
moderate risk

The Medal for
Meritorious Conduct
For especially meritorious
conduct not involving
heroism or risk of life.

While you have the option of remaining a Scout until your 16th birthday, at 14 you can choose to become a member of a Venturer company. Venturers, who are typically 14-17 years old, are largely responsible for planning and running their own programs and activities. The Venturer Motto, "Challenge", should give you some idea of the Venturer program's focus and nature.

As you approach your 14th birthday, contact a local Venturer company and join them in some of their activities. If there is no Venturer company in your area, speak to your Patrol Counsellor about how you and some of your friends might start your own company. For more information about Venturing, take a look at a copy of the *Canadian Venturer Handbook*.

CHALLENGE BADGES AND AWARDS

The round badges are called Challenge Badges. You can earn more than 45 of them. Requirements for the Challenge Badges generally ask you to work alone rather than with members of your patrol.

Why are the badges called "Challenge?" If you can already do a broad jump of 3 metres, is it a challenge to broad jump 1.5 metres? The challenge is to set yourself a goal beyond the 3 metres you know you can jump. Challenge Badges "challenge" you to explore areas of interest beyond what you can do now.

Of course, you can work on Challenge Badges where you already have a skill or an interest. Your challenge in those badges will be to complete them by doing your very best. Many of the first Challenge Badges you earn will probably relate to hobbies, interests, or sports in which you are already involved.

Suppose you want to accept the challenge of working on a Challenge Badge that looks interesting, but it's in an area that you know little or nothing about? How do you go about earning that badge? With the help of your Patrol Counsellor or your parents, guardians, or friends, you should first find a "resource person" who can help you with the badge's requirements.

For example, suppose you want to earn the Computer Challenge Badge, but don't own a computer. How can you earn it? Your first step will be to find a resource person. Ask Scouts in your patrol if any of them could be a resource person, or if they know someone who might volunteer. Look to see if others in the troop already have the Computer Challenge Badge, and ask them who they used as a resource person. Ask your Patrol Counsellor for suggestions. Your teachers at school might also know of someone. Almost always, your questions will lead to the name of a resource person who has the necessary skills and knowledge to help.

Once you've found the resource person, describe the general requirements, and ask if he or she will guide and help you to complete it. If you have looked over the Challenge Badges, you will have noticed that they generally don't list detailed requirements. It's up to you and your resource person to determine the exact requirements, keeping in mind that earning the badge should be a challenge.

When you complete the badge to the satisfaction of your resource person, he or she will notify your Patrol Counsellor so arrangements can be made for someone to present the badge to you at a troop meeting. Perhaps your resource person will even make the badge presentation.

You can earn each Challenge Badge only once. Although you may collect both stamps and coins, or have both a cat and a dog, you can earn only one Collector Challenge Badge, and only one Pet Care Badge. You wear Challenge Badges on your sash.

Challenge Awards recognize the number of Challenge Badges you have earned.

SCOUTS CANADA PROGRAM AND FORMAL ACTIVITY UNIFORM OPTIONS

OPTION 1
PROGRAM AND FORMAL UNIFORM

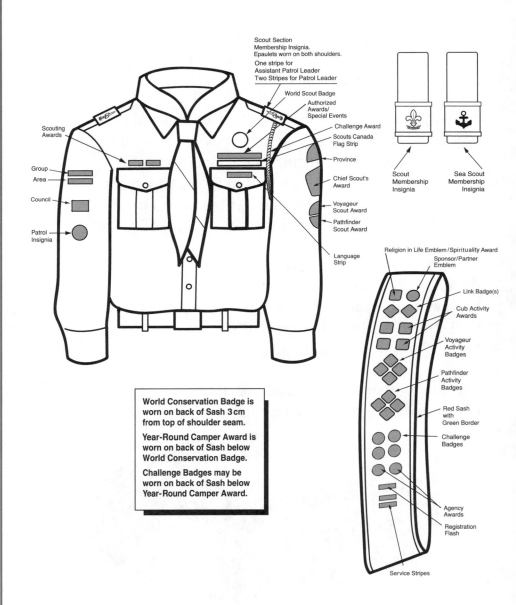

Scout Section
Membership Insignia.
Epaulets worn on both shoulders.
One stripe for
Assistant Patrol Leader
Two Stripes for Patrol Leader

World Scout Badge

Authorized
Awards/
Special Events

Challenge Award

Scouts Canada
Flag Strip

Province

Chief Scout's
Award

Voyageur
Scout Award

Pathfinder
Scout Award

Language
Strip

Scouting
Awards

Group

Area

Council

Patrol
Insignia

Scout
Membership
Insignia

Sea Scout
Membership
Insignia

Religion in Life Emblem / Spirituality Award

Sponsor/Partner
Emblem

Link Badge(s)

Cub Activity
Awards

Voyageur
Activity
Badges

Pathfinder
Activity
Badges

Red Sash
with
Green Border

Challenge
Badges

Agency
Awards

Registration
Flash

Service Stripes

World Conservation Badge is worn on back of Sash 3 cm from top of shoulder seam.

Year-Round Camper Award is worn on back of Sash below World Conservation Badge.

Challenge Badges may be worn on back of Sash below Year-Round Camper Award.

OPTION 2 PROGRAM UNIFORM

Program Uniform	
Official T-Shirt	Green, Grey or Orange
Footwear	Free Choice
Pants	Navy Blue or Tan
Shorts	Navy Blue or Tan
Vest	Green and Black Fleece
Sash	Optional
Necker	Group or National - if appropriate

OR

OPTION 2 FORMAL UNIFORM

Formal Uniform	
Shirt/Blouse*	White
Tie	Official Blue
Footwear	Black or Brown Shoes
Pants/ Skirt/Dress*	Navy Blue or Tan
Shorts	Navy Blue or Tan
Sash	Optional
Necker	No

* Female members
Note: Female members may substitute the section lapel pin for the tie.

OR

THE CHALLENGE AWARDS

Challenge Awards are different coloured lanyards that you wear around the left shoulder of the tan uniform only, with the ends tucked into the left pocket.

Any six (6) Challenge Badges from at least two (2) categories earn you the brown lanyard.

A total of 10 Challenge Badges from at least four (4) categories qualifies you for the green lanyard.

You need 14 Challenge Badges from at least six (6) categories to earn the white lanyard. Wear only the highest Challenge Award you have achieved.

MY PLAN FOR THE CHALLENGE AWARDS

On pages 127-8, pencil in the names of the badges you plan to earn. Change the pencil to ink when you have earned the badges, and write down the date.

BROWN (6 BADGES IN AT LEAST 2 CATEGORIES)

1. Badge —————————————————————

   Category —————————————————————

2. Badge —————————————————————

   Category —————————————————————

3. Badge —————————————————————

   Category —————————————————————

4. Badge —————————————————————

   Category —————————————————————

5. Badge —————————————————————

   Category —————————————————————

6. Badge —————————————————————

   Category —————————————————————

GREEN (10 BADGES IN AT LEAST 4 CATEGORIES)

7. Badge _____

   Category _____

8. Badge _____

   Category _____

9. Badge _____

   Category _____

10. Badge _____

    Category _____

WHITE (14 BADGES IN AT LEAST 6 CATEGORIES)

11. Badge _____

    Category _____

12. Badge _____

    Category _____

13. Badge _____

    Category _____

14. Badge _____

    Category _____

CHALLENGE BADGES

SCOUT CHALLENGE BADGES — ATHLETICS

Note: Participation in one particular sport can only apply to one badge in this category.

Individual Sport

Purpose: Demonstrate ability in an individual sport approved by your troop.

Requirements:

O 1. Be active in a sport that relies primarily on your individual effort and skill.

O 2. Show that you understand the rules, safety precautions and sportsmanship connected with the sport.

O 3. Discuss how your own skill in the sport can be improved, and create a self-improvement plan.

I received my **Individual Sport Badge** on (Date) _____

Swimming

Purpose: Demonstrate an ability to swim.

Requirements:

O 1. Demonstrate your swimming ability
in accordance with the Red Cross
"Swim Kids" Level 10 or Lifesaving Society Star Patrol.

OR

O 2. Complete all of the following:

   a) Tread water in deep water for a
   minimum of four (4) minutes;

   b) Front crawl for 100 metres;

   c) Back crawl for 100 metres;

   d) Elementary backstroke for 50 metres;

   e) Breaststroke for 50 metres;

   f) Sidestroke for 50 metres;

   g) Butterfly stroke, 3 x 10 metres; and

   h) Endurance swim for 400 metres
   continuously, using any stroke or
   combination of strokes.

I received my **Swimming Badge**
from _____ on
(Date) _____

Team Sport

Purpose: Demonstrate your ability in any suitable or appropriate team sport that is approved by your troop.

Requirements:

O 1. Be a member in good standing of a team for a full season.

O 2. Show by your participation in a team sport that you understand the rules, safety requirements, and sportsmanship connected with that sport.

O 3. Discuss how your own skill in the sport can be improved.

I received my **Team Sport Badge**
from _____ on _____
(Date) _____

Water Sport

Purpose: Demonstrate your ability in any water sport approved by your troop.

Requirements:

O 1. Be a regular participant in a water sport activity. For team water sports, demonstrate participation for a full season.

O 2. Show by your participation that you understand the rules, safety precautions, and sportsmanship connected with the sport.

O 3. Discuss how your own skill in the sport can be improved.

I received my **Water Sport Badge**
from _____ on
(Date) _____

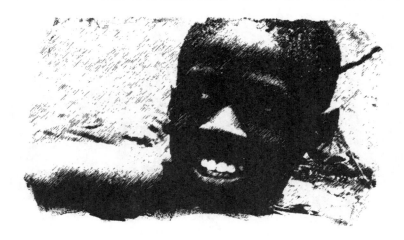

Winter Sport

Purpose: Demonstrate your ability in any suitable or appropriate winter sport that is approved by your troop.

Requirements:

○ 1. Participate in your chosen sport for a full winter season.

○ 2. Show by your participation in a winter sport that you understand the rules, safety requirements, and sportsmanship connected with that sport.

○ 3. Discuss how your own skill in the sport can be improved.

I received my **Winter Sport Badge**
from _____ on
(Date) _____

OUTDOORS

Advanced Tripping

Purpose: Demonstrate extended lightweight camping skills while adhering to Leave No Trace philosophies.

Requirements:

O 1. Complete twelve (12) nights of camping with at least two, three-night camping experiences. These must provide the opportunity to demonstrate advanced lightweight camping skills.

O 2. Demonstrate your ability to plan and prepare nutritious lightweight menus for an extended trip.

O 3. Demonstrate how to use appropriate lightweight equipment.

O 4. Demonstrate your ability to pack and carry your equipment.

O 5. Earn at least two (2) of the following badges: Pioneering, Exploring, Winter Scouting, Water Tripping, or Year-Round Camper.

○ 6. Instruct other Scouts or Cubs in lightweight camping skills.

○ 7. Lead a patrol camp.

○ 8. Demonstrate an understanding of environmental camping concerns.

I received my **Advanced Tripping Badge** from _____ on (Date) _____

Exploring

Purpose: Scouts should explore an unfamiliar area.

Requirements:

○ 1. Plan, conduct and evaluate three expeditions of increasing challenge, by foot, bike, canoe, etc. The distance and degree of difficulty will be determined with your Scouter, based on personal ability.

○ 2. Demonstrate the use of a map and compass.

○ 3. Explain risk management for these trips, including necessary safety precautions.

○ 4. Evaluate your experience (including your use of Leave No Trace philosophies).

I received my **Exploring Badge**
from _____ on
(Date) _____

Paddling

Purpose: Demonstrate the skills and knowledge to safely handle a canoe, kayak or similar craft on flat or slow moving water.

Note: You must wear a properly fitted PFD while in a boat.

Requirements:

Safety

O 1. Explain safety in, on and around water.

O 2. Properly select and wear a suitable PFD or life jacket. Explain your choice, and how it applies to Scouts Canada's regulations.

O 3. Demonstrate the use of a rescue-line throwing assist and an additional reaching or throwing assist.

O 4. Explain and demonstrate self-rescue (i.e. swim canoe ashore).

O 5. Explain and demonstrate canoe-over-canoe rescue.

Knowledge

O 1. Name and point out 10 parts on your craft, and 5 paddle parts.

○ 2. Explain the care and handling of your small craft, including launching and landing from a dock or shore.

○ 3. Explain how to avoid the following conditions, and their treatment:

    a) Hypothermia;

    b) Heat Exhaustion;

    c) Heat Stroke; and

    d) UV ray exposure.

○ 4. Know the Transport Canada regulations that apply to your small craft.

Skills

○ 1. Paddle equally well in bow and stern or, if your craft requires, solo.

○ 2. Demonstrate the stability of your craft (i.e. rock it vigorously).

○ 3. Pivot your craft 360 degrees in both directions.

○ 4. Paddle in a straight line for 100 metres.

○ 5. Demonstrate the following strokes as they apply to your craft: forward bow stroke, "J" stroke, stopping, sweep, reverse paddling, draw, and pry.

○ 6. Paddle a distance of 10 kilometres.

I received my **Paddling Badg**e
from _____ on
(Date) _____

Pioneering

Purpose: This badge recognizes the ability of a Scout in the area of pioneering. The ability goes beyond a basic knowledge of knots and lashing, to the point that the Scout can create useful and creative items using easily obtained wooden poles and rope (including cord and string).

Requirements:

O 1. Demonstrate the ability to tie three (3) knots not covered during the Voyageur requirements. Know the uses of the knots in a pioneering setting (e.g. clove hitch for beginning, and ending a lashing).

O 2. Prepare a demonstration illustrating square lashing, diagonal and tripod lashing, and indicate the uses of each.

○ 3. In a field setting and using only wooden poles and ropes (or other bindings), the Scout will construct any two of the following:

   a) a bridge type project;

   b) a camp gate, free standing flag pole or other useful item; or

   c) an entertainment type project (e.g. turnstile, swing, etc.)

I received my **Pioneering Badge**
from _____ on
(Date) _____

Powercraft

Purpose: To encourage Scouts to practise the safe operation of a powercraft, and be able to demonstrate basic maintenance.

Note: Everyone must wear a properly fitted PFD while in a boat.

Requirements:

◯ 1. Earn the Canadian Power Squadron Boat-Pro Award.

◯ 2. Demonstrate all skills required by the Boat-Pro Award.

◯ 3. Know the safety equipment required for your craft by Fisheries and Oceans (Canadian Coast Guard) and explain how to use it.

I received my **Powercraft Badge**
from _____ on
(Date) _____

Sailing

Purpose: This badge covers sailboats, dinghies and keelboats.

Note: Everyone must wear a properly fitted PFD while in a boat.

Requirements:

○ 1. Have at least the Canadian Red Cross Society's AquaQuest 7 or Small Craft Safety Survival Level, or the YMCA's Star IV Award, or demonstrate the following:

   a) Safety knowledge in, and on, water;

   b) From shore, a dock and from a boat, throw a reaching assist, a throwing assist (no line) and a throwing assist (with line) to someone in difficulty two metres from yourself. Bring the casualty to safety and security, talking to the casualty throughout to calm him;

   c) While fully clothed and wearing a PFD, jump into deep water, tread water for five minutes without signs of stress, and then swim 100 metres using any stroke;

   d) Demonstrate the HELP/huddle positions as used in and out of the water; and

   e) Show how to contact emergency services.

O 2. Properly select and wear a PFD.

O 3. Demonstrate the appropriate use of the safety equipment required for your craft by Fisheries and Oceans (Canadian Coast Guard).

O 4. a) Name and point out 25 parts of the hull and fittings, rigging, and sail;

b) Explain the difference between the following types of boats: cat-rigged, dinghy, sailboard, keelboat, and catamaran;

c) Demonstrate knowledge of proper procedures of care, maintenance and storage of your craft, and personal equipment.

○ 5. a) Demonstrate the proper methods of launching and landing a boat at a dock and shoreline. Demonstrate starting and stopping a motor, if applicable;

   b) Correctly rig and de-rig your vessel.

○ 6. a) Understand the basic concepts that affect boat stability;

   b) Demonstrate stability of the boat by vigorously rocking it for 30 seconds.

○ 7. a) Demonstrate safe entry and exit from a sailing craft, and changing of positions in a safe manner;

   b) Demonstrate how to right a capsized boat, if applicable;

   c) Know how to tie the following knots, and know what they are used for: reef, figure 8, round turn and two half hitches, bowline, rolling hitch, and sheetbend;

d) Properly secure the vessel to a dock by the bow or/and by the bow and stern, using any extra lines required for weather conditions.

○ 8. With adult guidance, demonstrate the following:

a) Manoeuvre your boat to and from a dock, mooring and a beach;

b) Sail a boat on both tacks;

c) Sail a beam reach on both tacks;

d) Sail a run on both tacks without gybing;

e) Demonstrate how to tack and gybe in both directions.

○ 9. a) Knowledge of Scouts Canada's watercraft regulations (as described in *B.P.&P.*);

b) Create and use a float plan; and

c) Knowledge of potentially dangerous waters in your area.

I received my **Sailing Badge** from _____ on (Date) _____

Water Tripping

Purpose: Experience all aspects of extended water trips.

Prerequisite: One of: Paddling Badge, Sailing Badge or Powercraft Badge.

Requirements:

○ 1. Help in the planning, and participate in, a three (3) day water trip adhering to Leave No Trace philosophies.

○ 2. Properly select and wear a PFD.

○ 3. Understand and explain the importance of a float plan.

○ 4. Demonstrate the ability to select the proper equipment for your trip.

○ 5. Demonstrate and explain ways to weatherproof camping gear.

○ 6. Demonstrate your skills at making emergency repairs to your tripping equipment.

○ 7. Show skills in map and compass reading, estimation of appropriate time and distance goals.

○ 8. Show weather observation skills.

○ 9. Demonstrate how to load your craft for tripping.

I received my **Water Tripping Badge**
from _____ on
(Date) _____

Weather

Purpose: To develop an interest in,
and skills about, weather
information.

Requirements:

O 1. Maintain an interest in weather by
recording for a one month period the
following weather data for a specific site:

a) Maximum temperature;

b) Minimum temperature;

c) Total 24-hour precipitation;

d) Mean wind direction and speed;

e) Barometric pressure and tendency at
the same time each day; and

f) Brief description of the weather for
the day.

O 2. Using a current weather map, such as those
found in a newspaper (or other source):

a) Identify and label a high pressure area,
a low pressure area, a warm front, and
a cold front;

b) Point out one location that is presently
affected by each of the above; and

c) Point out one location where the wind direction clearly shows Buys-Ballots Law and the speed related to the pressure gradient.

○ 3. For any two of the following, what advice would you give to your patrol if the forecast indicated that you could expect this type of weather where you are planning to go:

a) Lake-effect snow;

b) Chinook winds;

c) Blizzard or high windchill values;

d) Tornado;

e) Water spouts;

f) Dust devils;

g) Nor'easter winds in Atlantic Canada.

○ 4. For two outdoor outings by your patrol or troop:

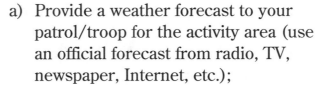

a) Provide a weather forecast to your patrol/troop for the activity area (use an official forecast from radio, TV, newspaper, Internet, etc.);

b) Advise members of the equipment required because of the forecast;

c) Maintain a weather log of temperature, precipitation and wind during the outing. You should make at least six (6) observations per day; and

d) After your outing, report to your patrol/troop how the weather affected the event.

I received my **Weather Badge**
from _____ on
(Date) _____

White Water

Purpose: Teach the safe and responsible handling of a canoe, kayak or similar craft in moving water.

Note: Everyone must wear a properly fitted PFD while in a boat. The Paddling Badge is a prerequisite for this badge

Requirements:

O 1. Describe the effects of rocker, wind, river current, and load positioning (including paddlers) on the craft.

O 2. Discuss the following parts of a rapid: sweeper, keeper, souse hole, haystack, roller, whirlpool, eddy, deep water V, submerged rock, areas of strong current, and eddy line. Discuss the importance of scouting out a rapid before entering it.

O 3. Select and wear a properly fitted PFD and helmet.

Suitable Equipment

O 1. Discuss provincial regulations relating to PFDs, and demonstrate proper use.

O 2. Discuss the importance of wearing a helmet.

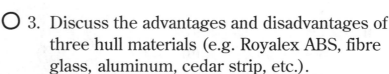

O 3. Discuss the advantages and disadvantages of three hull materials (e.g. Royalex ABS, fibre glass, aluminum, cedar strip, etc.).

O 4. When would a wet or dry suit be necessary?

O 5. Demonstrate accurate throwing with a throw bag.

O 6. Demonstrate appropriate footwear.

Paddle Strokes

In moving water demonstrate an effective:

O 1. High brace;

O 2. Low brace;

O 3. Sideslip left and right;

O 4. Back paddling;

O 5. Eddy in and eddy out on the left and right;

O 6. Upstream ferry left and right; and

O 7. Downstream ferry left and right.

General Knowledge

O 1. Demonstrate what to do if capsized.

O 2. From the International River Classification System, describe Class 1, 2, 3 rapids.

○ 3. Considering your skill level, strength and the type of equipment you are using, what would make a rapid unrunable for you?

I received my **White Water Badge**
from _____ on
(Date) _____

Winter Scouting

Purpose: Demonstrate in the winter an ability to hike and camp in the outdoors adhering to Leave No Trace philosophies.

Requirements:

○ 1. Plan and conduct three winter activities, one of which must be an overnight camp.

○ 2. Demonstrate appropriate gear suitable for winter camping.

○ 3. Know the signs and first aid for hypothermia, frostbite, and snow blindness.

○ 4. Prepare a winter survival kit.

○ 5. Demonstrate a knowledge of good meals suitable for winter activities.

○ 6. Lay and light a fire.

O 7. Show how to avoid, and what to do about, the following:

a) Breaking through ice;

b) Carbon monoxide poisoning;

c) Frostbite;

d) Becoming lost in winter conditions;

e) Getting caught in a blizzard;

f) Snow blindness;

g) Skin stuck to cold metal;

h) Hypothermia; and

i) Wet clothing.

I received my **Winter Scouting Badge**
from _____ on
(Date) _____

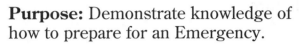

HOME & FAMILY

Emergency Preparedness

Purpose: Demonstrate knowledge of how to prepare for an Emergency.

Requirements:

◯ 1. Describe three situations that would lead to a community emergency. Describe how emergencies can affect the local community and the people in it.

◯ 2. a) Create/update a Family Emergency Plan and discuss with your family.

b) As a patrol, create a Troop Emergency Plan and present it to your troop. The Court of Honour will agree on the final Troop Emergency Plan.

◯ 3. Create/Update an Emergency Survival Kit for home use (to support your family for 72 hours).

◯ 4. Identify a person in the community who would possibly require help in an emergency (e.g. someone with special needs, a senior) and how you could assist them.

◯ 5. List three emergencies that are created by climate/weather. What would you do to prepare and react to those?

◯ 6. Earn the First Aid Badge.

I received my **Emergency Preparedness Badge**
from _____ on _____
(Date) _____

Builder

Purpose: Show an interest in building objects.

Requirements:

○ 1. Build at least two objects from scratch, not using pre-cut or pre-formed kits.

○ 2. Demonstrate the safe handling of materials and tools used in your project.

I received my **Builder Badge**
from _____ on
(Date) _____

Cooking

Purpose: Show an interest in planning and cooking nutritious meals.

Requirements:

O 1. a) Demonstrate a knowledge of the food groups outlined in the Canada Food Guide;

    b) Give examples of foods in each food group, including information on the energy and nutritional values, and their effects on the body; and

    c) Explain the importance of three balanced meals a day, as well as the body's daily need for fluid intake.

O 2. Demonstrate a knowledge of appropriate hygiene practices associated with meal preparation, and clean-up after a meal.

O 3. Prepare a menu for your patrol for a weekend camp. Discuss with your patrol the reasons for your menu choices, such as nutritional values, ease of preparation, variety, and transportation.

O 4. Demonstrate a knowledge of safety requirements associated with cooking appliances and food storage, used both in the home and outdoors.

○ 5. Prepare a menu, and cook a meal for your patrol outdoors.

○ 6. Prepare a menu, and cook a meal for your family at home.

I received my **Cooking Badge**
from _____ on
(Date) _____

Family Care

Purpose: Show an interest in personal responsibility for your family.

Requirements:

○ 1. Show that you are able to look after yourself, your home, and your family for a short period of time.

    a) Be able to safely operate the appliances in your home (e.g. stove, microwave, oven, vacuum, washing machine, etc.);

    b) Be able to plan, purchase, and prepare a meal;

    c) Keep your home neat and clean.

○ 2. Explain, and be able to carry out, the daily routine of running your family home (i.e. wake-up time, meal time, family chores, bed time, etc.).

○ 3. Because family sickness may be the reason you'll have to look after the home, show that you have a general knowledge how to look after sick people. Also, show that you know the principles of personal cleanliness, and home sanitation.

Note: Satisfactory completion of a "Babysitting Course" or a "Home Nursing" course will qualify you for this badge.

I received my **Family Care Badge**
from _____ on
(Date) _____

Home Repair

Purpose: Demonstrate the ability to make home repairs.

Requirements:

O 1. Be able to identify trouble, (e.g. leaking faucet) and make the necessary repairs to four home projects, two of which will reduce the amount of heat escaping from your home (e.g. caulking windows).

O 2. Demonstrate the safety precautions required for each project.

O 3. Show how to safely operate and maintain any three hand tools, and any two power tools used in your home repair projects.

O 4. In all projects, demonstrate that you have finished the job in a competent manner, and have cleaned up the tools and the job site.

I received my **Home Repair Badge**
from _____ on
(Date) _____

CLIMATE CHANGE CHALLENGE
DÉFI CHANGEMENT CLIMATIQUE (See Page 213.)

Pet Care

Purpose: Show an interest and ability in maintaining a healthy pet.

Requirements:

○ 1. Look after a pet for at least six months.

○ 2. Show the required feeding, grooming, exercise, affection, and training that a specific pet needs.

○ 3. Know the laws in your community that apply to keeping a pet.

○ 4. Show that you understand what is considered cruelty to animals.

○ 5. Explain the different health risks associated with wild animals versus domesticated pets.

○ 6. Visit a veterinary hospital, or equivalent, to learn about active and preventive services available to your pet.

I received my **Pet Care Badge**
from _____ on
(Date) _____

Safety

Purpose: Demonstrate a knowledge of safety.

Requirements:

O 1. Show how to get help (e.g. from police, firefighters, ambulance).

O 2. Explain the different classes of fires, and how to use different types of fire extinguishers.

O 3. Demonstrate the safety aspects, and differences between fuses and circuit breakers.

O 4. Show what to do if a fire starts. Plan escape routes for your home or meeting place. Know where fire extinguishers and smoke alarms are located.

O 5. Make a list of fire hazards in your home and meeting place.

O 6. Demonstrate how and why you should store medicines, cleaning aids and flammable materials. Be able to identify the hazard symbols.

O 7. Demonstrate basic "Rules of the Road" for bicycling.

O 8. Show how to avoid and treat carbon monoxide poisoning.

O 9. Identify common poisonous plants in your area, and how to treat symptoms.

I received my **Safety Badge**
from _____ on
(Date) _____

PERSONAL DEVELOPMENT

Collector

Purpose: Show an interest in putting a collection together.

Requirements:

○ 1. Own and add to a collection that you have worked on for the last six months. This must have been done as a Scout.

2. Display your collection in a suitable manner.

3. Present your collection, your interest in it, some of its history and describe why and how you chose to display it as you have.

I received my **Collector Badge**
from _____ on
(Date) _____

Communicator

Purpose: Demonstrate formal communication skills.

Requirements:

Complete one of the following:

O   1. Serve on the editorial or writing staff of a magazine or paper for at least eight (8) months, or during the time two (2) issues are published. Show that you were able to rewrite and improve an article or manuscript, while still retaining important information. Write at least two (2) articles.

O   2. As secretary for your Court of Honour or other troop/patrol meetings, keep records and minutes for at least six (6) months.

O   3. Take part in two organized debates or two public speaking events. Discuss the preparations for your part in these events.

I received my **Communicator Badge**
from _____ on
(Date) _____

Individual Specialty

First Aid

Purpose: Demonstrate a knowledge of first aid procedures.

Requirements:

○ 1. Earn the St. John Ambulance First Aid Standard level, or equivalent Red Cross level.

OR

○ 2. Demonstrate to a trained instructor the techniques and knowledge equivalent to First Aid Standard level.

I received my **First Aid Badge**
from _____ on
(Date) _____

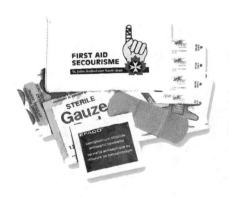

Purpose: To provide a way to recognize a Scout who has a special interest.

Requirements:

○ 1. A Scout may propose a subject and requirements for this badge, or may develop them in cooperation with other troop members. The requirements should be presented to the patrol meeting or Court of Honour for review.

○ 2. Topics selected for this badge should not be covered in any other Challenge Badge.

○ 3. The Scout leader must send a copy of the badge requirements to the local Scout council for information.

○ 4. A Scout may hold only one Individual Specialty Badge at a time.

○ 5. A Scout may choose a new Individual Specialty once a year.

Note to leaders: Make sure the requirements challenge the individual's abilities. Remember that the purpose of the badge is to recognize the best effort of the Scout.

I received my **Individual Specialty Badge** from _____ on (Date) _____

CLIMATE CHANGE CHALLENGE
DÉFI CHANGEMENT CLIMATIQUE (See Page 216.)

Language Strip

Purpose: Demonstrate an ability to speak in another language.

Requirements:

O 1. Show you know a language other than your own by talking on a subject of your choice for 15 minutes.

O 2. The person to whom you are speaking or reporting to must agree that your pronunciation, grammar, and spelling are basically correct and age-appropriate.

I received my **Language Strip**
from _____ on
(Date) _____

Lifesaving

Purpose: To demonstrate knowledge of lifesaving techniques with various types of victims.

Requirements:

O 1. Earn the Bronze Star of the Lifesaving Society.

OR

O 2. To the satisfaction of a qualified instructor, complete the following:

   a) Know how to treat and prevent further shock in a victim;

   b) Be able to identify unconscious and injured victims;

   c) Demonstrate the HELP position with a PFD or other swimming aids for three minutes;

   d) Demonstrate the front survival position for three minutes;

   e) Demonstrate the "egg beater kick." (Your Scout may use arms for support);

f) Enter the water in the "stride" position, maintaining eye contact with the victim;

g) Enter the water as though for a rescue using maximum speed (shallow dive);

h) Show how you would avoid being grasped from the front and the rear by a drowning victim;

i) Remove an unconscious victim from the water, helped by an assistant. (The assistant should know as much as the rescuer);

j) Rescue a non-breathing victim. Provide rescue breathing until you are relieved of responsibility. Demonstrate care once the victim starts to breathe on his or her own;

k) Provide support for a weak or injured non-swimmer, with minimum risk to the rescuer. Provide care until relieved of responsibility;

l) Provide assistance to a weak or poor swimmer in deep water with a non-buoyant aid, while avoiding high risk to the rescuer. Provide care until relieved of responsibility; and

m) Swim 400 metres continuously. Do not use the "resting" stroke.

I received my **Lifesaving Badg**e
from _____ on
(Date) _____

Troop Specialty

Purpose: To provide a way to recognize a troop that has a special interest.

Requirements:

O 1. The troop will identify the requirements for this badge.

O 2. The Scout leader must send a copy of the badge requirements to the local Scout council for information.

O 3. A troop may have only one Specialty Badge at a time.

O 4. A troop may change its Specialty Badge once a year if it wishes.

Note: Make sure the requirements challenge the abilities of those in the troop. Use the idea-generating power of your patrol meeting and Court of Honour to come up with ideas for your Troop Specialty Badge.

I received my **Troop Specialty Badge**
from _____ on
(Date) _____

CLIMATE CHANGE CHALLENGE
DÉFI CHANGEMENT CLIMATIQUE (See Page 216.)

SCIENCE & TECHNOLOGY

Computer

Purpose: Demonstrate
your understanding
of computers.

PART A — KNOWLEDGE

O 1. Define and explain the
function of each of the following:

❏ CPU (central processing unit),	❏ mouse,
	❏ floppy disk,
❏ RAM,	❏ CD rom,
❏ ROM,	❏ tape drive,
❏ printer,	❏ scanner,
❏ disk drive,	❏ digital camera,
❏ monitor,	❏ speakers,
❏ keyboard,	❏ modem,
❏ hard disk,	❏ data projector.
❏ joy stick,	

O 2. Describe how a computer memory/floppy
disk/CD-ROM (select one) stores information
(e.g. text, images, audio and video).

O 3. Describe the World Wide Web and how
computers around the world access it.

Part B – Proficiency

Do four of the following:

O 1. Use either a database or spreadsheet program
to create a roster of your troop showing the

name, address and telephone number of each Scout, as well as a record of each Scout's attendance for the past month.

O 2. Use a spreadsheet program to develop the budget for a weekend camp for your troop or patrol. This spreadsheet should show both budget and actual amounts for each item, as well as the difference between the two.

O 3. Use a word processor to write a letter to the parents of each troop member, inviting them to a special meeting night. Include a graphic in it, and, if possible, use mail merge to personalize each letter.

O 4. Use a computer graphics program to design and draw a campsite plan for your troop.

O 5. Using web authoring software, design and create a web site for your troop. Include at least two pages, one graphic, a link to Scouts Canada (www.scouts.ca), and an email link to an approved adult in your troop.

O 6. Use a word processing or publishing program to create a 3-column pamphlet which would publicize your troop to senior Cubs or newcomers to Scouts. Include the logo of your troop, planned activities for the year, names and phone numbers of leaders, and an invitation to join.

O 7. Use a camera and a scanner or a digital camera to take pictures of an outing or special event involving your troop. Then, using media presentation software, put together a presentation (include photos, captions and, if possible, sound) that your troop can use at a "parents' night" or a linking activity with a Cub pack.

O 8. Locate five troops in other parts of Canada that have a home page. Explain the process, including the name(s) of the search engine(s) you used to locate the troops. Email each of them, explaining that you are completing your Computer badge, and invite them to send a greeting to your troop or patrol. On a map of Canada, pinpoint the locations of the troops.

O 9. Use a computer to connect to the World Wide Web and a search engine to locate information on a Scouting topic related to the content of a Scout badge or award. Download and save the information, and print it out. If you believe that other Scouts would benefit from this information, email the URL to program@scouts.ca.

O 10. Use a programming language to write a program. The program should show examples of decision-making and looping. Prepare a write up of the steps you used to create and test the program.

Part C – Initiative

Do ONE of the following:

○ 1. Visit a business or industry that uses computers. Using a computer, prepare a report on how computers are being used in the site you visited, how they effect workers, and what future plans the business or industry has for computing.

○ 2. Describe four jobs in the computer field, including the necessary training for the jobs, and opportunities for these jobs in your area of Canada.

Part D – Ethics

Discuss with or explain to your patrol members or patrol counsellor, each of the following:

○ 1. Why it is not right to accept a burned copy of a purchased computer game or program from a friend.

○ 2. How to give credit to the authors of information that is downloaded from the World Wide Web, and what you should do if you want a copy of an image from the World Wide Web or a CD-ROM. (Background reading: http://www.communities.ca/e/copyright.html)

○ 3. The personal safety aspects involved in using email or chat rooms.

I received my **Computer Badge**
from _____ on
(Date) _____

Engineering

Purpose: Explore the fields of engineering. Some engineering fields include: aeronautical, aerospace, architectural, civil, computer, electrical, marine, mechanical, meteorological, and mining.

Requirements:

Complete one of the following:

O 1. Visit an industrial plant, an electricity generating plant, a food processing or packing plant, a sewage treatment plant, a mine, or another centre of engineering activity. Report on the visit, the equipment used, the end product of the process, and the good it does for the community. Include sketches, photos if possible, and a model or mock-up of the process to show that you understand the basic ideas involved. Detail what safety devices and regulations you noticed during your visit.

O 2. Show how to work and repair any one of the motor power energy sources such as internal combustion engines (gasoline or diesel), turbine drives, steam engines, rockets, or electric, wind, or water drives. Discuss the engineering principles involved, and show that you have a good knowledge of the safety measures required for the energy source.

○ 3. As a draftsperson, show that you can make scale drawings in third angle, orthographic projection (three views) of simple pieces of machinery or machine parts. Properly finish the drawings with border, title, and views described. Show examples of tracings you have done of an electrical or electronic circuit, an architectural drawing, or an engineering drawing. Discuss the merits of the various ways of copying these drawings for further use.

I received my **Engineering Badge**
from _____ on
(Date) _____

Purpose: Show an interest in the sciences. Some scientific fields include: archaeology, astronomy, biology, chemistry, electronics, geology, mathematics, medicine, physics, zoology, microbiology, botany, and biotechnology.

Requirements:

○ 1. Show by your participation in a science fair, exposition, open house, or private demonstration that you have an interest and skill in a scientific subject beyond the level expected of you in your school work. Demonstration by devices, models, charts, collections, or in the field, the aspect that interests you. Explain the background, and how it relates to the rest of the world or other fields of science.

I received my **Science Badge**
from _____ on
(Date) _____

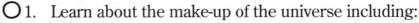

Space Exploration

Purpose: To encourage youth to investigate the area of space exploration.

Requirements:

Part A - Knowledge

◯ 1. Learn about the make-up of the universe including:
- its composition   - the earth
- the solar system   - space radiation
- the sun

   See: http://planetscapes.com/ or
   http://kids.msfc.nasa.gov/solarsystem.

◯ 2. Describe the principles associated with rocket propulsion. See:
   http://www.execpc.com/~culp/space/propulsn.html or
   http://users.commkey.net/Braeunig/space/propuls.htm.

◯ 3. Demonstrate knowledge of the different types of space vehicles. See:
   http://www.spacefuture.com/vehicles/vehicles.shtml

◯ 4. Creatively describe the following:
- Kepler's Law
   (http//www.cvc.org/science/kepler.htm)
- Newton's Law
   (http://www.aloha.com/~isaac/3laws/3laws.htm)
- how an orbit works
   (http://www.execpc.com/~culp/space/orbit.html)
- the types of orbits
   http://users.commkey.net/Braeunig/space/orbmech.htm#types

○ 5. Understand basic satellite designs. See:

http://www.spacefuture.com/vehicles/designs.shtml or

http://www.thetech.org/hyper/satellite/

○ 6. Describe the major moments in Canadian space history. See:

http://www.space.gc.ca/asc/eng/about/csa-organisation/csm.asp

Part B - Proficiency

○ 1. Make a list of the different ways in which we utilize space today. See:

http://www.thetech.org/hyper/satellite/

○ 2. Design a rocket or satellite, and explain its parts. See:

http://www.execpc.com/~culp/space/rckt_asm.jpg or

http://www.thetech.org/hyper/satellite/

Part C - Initiative

○ 1. Visit an agency associated with space exploration (e.g. museum, web site). See:

http://www.space.gc.ca/asc.index.html or

http://www.hq.nasa.gov/

○ 2. Describe, including the educational requirements needed for, four jobs related to the space industry.

* We provide Web Sites only as a suggestion.

I received my **Space Exploration Badge**

from _____ on

(Date) _____

CULTURE & SOCIETY

Artist

Purpose: To recognize an interest and participation in art.

Requirements:

○ 1. Show that you have an interest in, and have practised, an art form such as graphic art (drawing or painting), modelling, pottery, sculpture, etc.

○ 2. Explain the characteristics and properties of the material you used (e.g. plastic, wood, clay).

○ 3. Demonstrate and explain the use of the tools and equipment used for your art form.

○ 4. Show three pieces of your finished artwork.

I received my **Artist Badge**
from _____ on
(Date) _____

Cultural Awareness

Purpose: To gain a greater understanding of Canada's
cultural diversity.

Requirements:

○ 1. Learn about a cultural group of people,
including what language they speak, their
traditions and spiritual beliefs.

○ 2. Lead an activity or game which is specific to
that culture.

○ 3. Prepare a food which is specific to that culture,
and share it with your patrol/troop.

I received my **Cultural Awareness Badge**
from _____ on
(Date) _____

Handicraft

Purpose: To recognize skill in some form of handicraft.

Requirements:

◯ 1. Show that you have an interest in, have practised, and gained skill in some form of handicraft, such as carving, decorating, embossing, stamping, weaving, needlecraft, etc.

◯ 2. Present recent examples of your work.

I received my **Handicraft Badge**
from _____ on
(Date) _____

Heritage

Purpose: To explore a Scout's heritage.

Requirements:

O 1. Show that you know where to find information about the heritage of your community by explaining:

    a) Primary and secondary sources;

    b) Oral and written sources; and

    c) The use of materials in archives, museums, and libraries.

O 2. Carry out one of the projects suggested below, and make an oral, written, or scrapbook presentation to your troop.

    a) Construct a family tree showing at least five generations;

    b) Give a report on the origins of your community or neighbourhood; and

    c) In a rural area, make a study of at least 30 early grave stones in the local cemetery. Give a presentation on these former residents and how they contributed to the area.

O 3. a) Outline the history of the World Scout Movement from its beginning, with special emphasis on the contribution of its founder; and

b) Give a brief history of your own Scout troop and district.

O 4. Choose an historic building, place, monument, park, structure, or organization in your area, and give a report on its history and importance.

O 5. Research and make a presentation on the history and legends of Native people in your area.

OR

O 6. Research and make a presentation of Native people in their present-day life.

I received my **Heritage Badge**
from _____ on
(Date) _____

Literary Arts

Purpose: To recognize participation in literary arts.

Requirements:

1. Show an interest in one or more of the literary arts by presenting and discussing some of your work in such fields as biography, drama, fiction, or poetry.

OR

O 2. Present reviews of books, plays, poems, radio, TV shows, or movies, and be prepared to discuss and defend your opinions.

I received my **Literary Arts Badge**

from _____ on

(Date) _____

Modeller

Purpose: To recognize interest and ability in constructing models or toys.

Requirements:

O 1. Show you have an interest in, have practised, and have gained skill in building models or toys. (Models may be produced from kits.)

O 2. Present three (3) recent examples of your work.

I received my **Modeller Badge**
from _____ on
(Date) _____

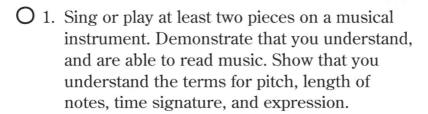

Music

Purpose: To recognize musical ability.

Requirements:

Do one of the following:

O 1. Sing or play at least two pieces on a musical instrument. Demonstrate that you understand, and are able to read music. Show that you understand the terms for pitch, length of notes, time signature, and expression.

OR

O 2. Be a regular member of a school, social, or church choir, or musical group, and take part in at least three performances.

I received my **Music Badge**
from _____ on
(Date) _____

Performing Arts

Purpose: To recognize participation in a performing art.

Requirements:

Show an interest in, and participate in, any one of the following:

O 1. Entertain an audience, either by yourself or with a small group, for at least 15 minutes with a varied program. It could include dance, role-playing, music, acting, storytelling, etc.

O 2. Rehearse and direct a small group in a play lasting 20 minutes.

O 3. Participate in a multi-act play, as an actor or stage crew with your school or theatre group.

I received my **Performing Arts Badge**
from _____ on
(Date) _____

Photography

Purpose: To recognize photography knowledge and skills.

Requirements:

O 1. Demonstrate and explain the use of your camera, video, or other.

O 2. Explain how your camera records an image, as well as the developing process, if appropriate.

O 3. Show examples of your work, describing the composition, choice of subject matter, and lighting and exposure.

I received my **Photography Badge**
from _____ on
(Date) _____

Special Needs Awareness

Purpose: To gain a greater awareness of special needs requirements.

Requirements:

○ 1. Meet with an agency or person providing support to persons with a special need, and learn about the support given. Lead an awareness exercise or game for that special need.

OR

○ 2. For at least three months, provide assistance with the ongoing support of a person with a special need.

I received my **Special Needs Awareness Badge** from _____ on (Date) _____

Agriculture

Purpose: Demonstrate your knowledge and involvement in an agricultural project.

Requirements:

O 1. Participate in, and be able to discuss, a planned agricultural project (e.g. beef cattle, bee keeping, poultry farming, tree farming, and cereal crops).

O 2. Keep a record of your project and explain to your patrol/troop the costs, profits, methods, results and suggestions for improvement. A successful completion of a 4H or horticulture club project will qualify for this badge.

I received my **Agriculture Badge** from _____ on (Date) _____

Fish & Wildlife

Purpose: Demonstrate your knowledge and involvement in fish and wildlife management.

Requirements:

O 1. Investigate and be able to discuss factors which effect fish or wildlife management. These include diseases, pollution, endangered species and habitat destruction, carry capacity and edge effect.

O 2. Find out how to obtain a hunting or fishing license, and discuss the value of regulations.

O 3. After consulting with local authorities, report to your troop on a fish or wildlife improvement project that you participated in. This might include restoring stream banks, planting stream cover, river bank clean-up, building nest boxes, helping to tag or band wildlife or adopting a park.

I received my **Fish & Wildlife Badge**
from _____ on
(Date) _____

Forestry

Purpose: Demonstrate your knowledge and involvement in forest management.

Requirements:

◯ 1. Investigate and be able to discuss forestry concerns, such as diseases, pest control, logging, product utilization, replanting, and fires.

◯ 2. Investigate and be able to discuss forest ecology such as forest types, factors of growth, the value to wildlife, and air quality.

◯ 3. Participate in, and report to your troop, on a forest improvement project such as Scoutrees, stand improvement, reforesting, or pest control.

I received my **Forestry Badge**
from _____ on
(Date) _____

Horticulture

Purpose: Demonstrate your knowledge and involvement in an horticultural project.

Requirements:

◯ 1. Plan, plant, and tend throughout one complete growing season (from early spring to early winter) a flower garden measuring at least 4 metres square.

OR

◯ 2. Plan, plant, and tend throughout one complete growing season (from early spring to early winter) a vegetable garden measuring at least 9 metres square.

OR

◯ 3. Plan, plant, and tend throughout one complete growing season (from early spring to early winter) a landscaped property measuring at least 16 metres square.

◯ 4. Explain:

a) Preparation of the soil;

b) Location of the plants;

c) Fertilization and mulching used;

d) The program of weeding, watering, and staking; and

e) The preparation for winter.

O 5. Explain your choice of plants and show or illustrate your results. Photographs, floral displays, horticultural exhibits, growth records, and produce are interesting ways to present your report.

I received my **Horticulture Badge**
from _____ on
(Date) _____

203

Naturalist

Purpose: Demonstrate your knowledge and skill in the field of natural science, emphasizing outdoor activity.

Requirements:

○ 1. In a presentation of your choosing, explain the meaning of balance of nature, migration, life cycle, niche, community, and food web.

○ 2. Identify 15 trees or shrubs, 10 non-woody plants, 10 birds, and 10 mammals native to your area.

In the field (if possible), identify 20 species in any category of your choice: mammals, reptiles, fish, plants, birds, trees, butterflies, moths, or other insects. Know the habitat, migratory patterns, distinctive behaviour, and life cycle of each species in the category you have chosen.

I received my **Naturalist Badge**
from _____ on
(Date) _____

Recycling

Purpose: Demonstrate your knowledge and involvement in recycling.

Requirements:

○ 1. Lead a discussion about the meaning of recycling, and describe why recycling has become more important in recent years.

○ 2. Report on the "recycling process" in your community. What happens to a tin can or bottle?

○ 3. a) Examine what you recycle at home to ensure you are recycling all items accepted by your municipality. Expand it to include items that can be donated (clothing) and refused (flyers, excess packaging).

OR

b) At a camp with members of your patrol, organize a recycling program for the duration of the camp, and deposit all recyclable materials at your local recycling centre. Document your program details, and share them with the camp administrator.

I received my **Recycling Badge**
from _____ on
(Date) _____

CLIMATE CHANGE CHALLENGE
DÉFI CHANGEMENT CLIMATIQUE (See Page 213.)

Soil & Water Management

Purpose: Demonstrate your knowledge and involvement in soil and water management.

Requirements:

O 1. Investigate and be able to discuss soil and water management concerns as they relate to soil erosion, food cycle, water cycle, and the water table.

O 2. Demonstrate different soil make-ups in your area, and describe the advantages and disadvantages of each.

O 3. Visit local farm lands, an industrial site, marsh areas, ponds or lakes, and describe their importance in relation to soil and water management.

I received my **Soil & Water Management Badge** from _____ on (Date) _____

INDEX

CLIMATE CHANGE CHALLENGE

* 1. Do three of the four following badges; Home Repair Badge; Recycling Badge; World Conservation Badge or Individual/ Troop Specialty Badge.

* 2. Make your home more energy wise: Reduce waste of precious energy resources, save your parents' money, and reduce your contribution to climate change. Investigate and reduce energy consumption in your home by following the Home Energy Audit and Online Energy Calculator posted on the Scouts Canada web site (*www.scouts.ca*).

* 3. Take the transportation challenge: Develop a personal transportation challenge. Actively pursue a sport that can serve as a mode of transportation (e.g. biking, in-line skating, skateboarding, etc.). Show that you understand the rules, safety and precautions connected with using the sport as a mode of transportation, as well as the advantages of it, including those of health, air quality and climate change. Make and pursue a plan to travel to one destination (of approximately 5 km) by this alternative mode of transportation once a week for a two month period.

* 4. Select and complete three of the challenges from the list below:

i) Find out all of the items that your municipality will accept for recycling. Examine what you recycle at home or at the home of your grandparents or another relative and expand your efforts to include all of these items. Don't forget about items that can be donated (e.g. clothing, dishes, etc.), repaired (e.g. resoling shoes) and refused (e.g. flyers, excess packaging, etc.). Find a way to help your family, relative or grandparent to recycle, reduce, reuse and refuse all these possible items.

ii) Report back to your patrol/troop leader on what you accomplished. This challenge also can help you to earn the Recycling badge.

iii) With permission and help from your parents, do at least two home repairs that will help to reduce the heat or air conditioning escaping from your home. Hint: doing the Home Energy Audit will give you some ideas on what kinds of repairs you can do to complete this challenge.
This challenge also can help you to earn the Home Repair badge.

iv) With your troop, do a program to educate people in your community about climate change. Develop your own program idea, or select one of these:

- Adopt a location in the community where cars are often seen idling (at a community mall, at school, outside individual stores, etc.). Idling wastes gas and puts pollutants and green house gases into the atmosphere. Launch a no-idling campaign to decrease or eliminate idling in this location. Take advantage of resources offered through Natural Resources Canada's Office of Energy Efficiency to assist you to develop and deliver the program (*http://oee.nrcan.gc.ca/transportation/personal/idling.cfm*).

- Organize a tire pressure clinic to help cars to run optimally. Visit http://*www.betiresmart.ca/* to find out more about this program and how you can organize a tire clinic in your community.

- Hold a community car wash to discourage people from using automated car washes. This will reduce the use of energy to run the automated car wash.

- Create and distribute flyers to help your community benefit from what you have learned about climate change. You can encourage them to recycle more items, to find and fix energy leaks in their own home, or to buy locally grown foods. Your project also can help you to earn the Troop Specialty Badge.

v) Complete a project that includes some recognizable work in your community or troop. For example, learn about the range of weather conditions that climate change may bring to your region and make a presentation giving advice on what precautions you would take for a camping-canoeing trip planned during in any one season (spring, summer or winter) or what precautions your community or city should take to prepare for the future. Make a presentation, display or report describing your project, and the global importance of the issue. You may complete the project as an individual or in a group. This challenge also can help you earn the World Conservation Badge.

vi) Show that you know how to make decisions that reduce the energy you use in running your family home including turning off unnecessary lights and appliances, reducing use of the clothes dryer by hanging laundry to dry, identifying and selecting local products to plan a meal, buying products with less packaging, etc. Track what you did and how often over a period of a month.

vii)   Participate in a Scoutrees project as an individual or with your troop and demonstrate your understanding of the link between trees and climate change. You could serve as a leader for a Beaver or Cub Scoutrees project and teaching them how Scoutrees work to reduce greenhouse gases.

The **Climate Change Challenge Crest** is **NOT** worn on any uniform or on the sash.

INDIVIDUAL/TROOP SPECIALTY BADGE (EXAMPLES)

* 1. After exploring ways to improve the energy efficiency of your home, educate others as to how they may improve their own homes (e.g. information booth; pamphlet, etc.). Provide estimates of the energy, money and GHGs saved by using an online calculator (*www.climatechange.gc.ca* or *www.scouts.ca*).

* 2. Adopt a location in the community where cars are often seen idling (school yard, sports facility) and launch a no-idling campaign to decrease idling in this location. Resources can be found at: *http://oee.nrcan.gc.ca/transportation/personal/idling.cfm*

* 3. Organize a tire pressure clinic. Visit *www.betiresmart.ca* to find out more about this program.

Scouts Canada would like to thank the following photographers who contributed pictures for this book:

Wayne Barrett	pages 2, 9, 24, 25
Chris Baxter	pages 69, 100
Jim Dicker	page 165
John Dicker	page 191
Heather Downs-MacIntosh	page 203
Benjamin Eng	page 94
Doug Erickson	page 91
Bruno Fafard	page iii
Sharon Fikkert	page 188
Amy Godwin	page 152
Judy Harcuss	page 5
"Greybeard"	page 123
Erik "Haggis" Hagborg	pages 6, 65, 98
Eric Harkonen	page 33
Margaret Keith	page 141
Bill Kowalchyk	page 97
Barrett & Mackay	pages 4, 53
Mark McDermitt	pages 38, 47
Lauren McKinnon	page 109
Peter Ng	page iii, 28, 30, 32
Martha Paris	page 13
Gary Parker	page 85
Kevin Paxton	page 23
George Pearce	pages 145, 146
Bonnie Phillips	page iii
Dennis Power	pages iii, 3, 7, 10, 16, 17, 18, 31, 36, 41, 68, 73, 87, 100, 116, 117, 125, 132, 133, 136, 194
Marty Schlosser	page 78
Ron Schmiedge	page iii
Peter K. Waycik	page 205
Ron Zimmerman	page 75

All other photographs from the Scouts Canada archives.